THE SECRET SIDE OF MONEY

THE SECRET SIDE OF MONEY
A HISTORY OF MANIPULATION

By
Dee Zahner

LTAA COMMUNICATIONS
PUBLISHERS
HESPERIA, CALIFORNIA

First Printing 1996

Copyright 1996 by Dee Zahner
All rights reserved

Published by
LTAA Communications
P.O. Box 403092
Hesperia, California 92345

Printed in the United States of America
Library of Congress Catalog Card Number: 95-90956
ISBN: 1-887017-02-X

To the many faithful and honest men and women who daily serve the public in the banking profession.

CONTENTS

Introduction ix

1. Ancient History of Money............................ 1
2. Early History of Banking.............................. 8
3. Rise of a Banking Dynasty.......................... 13
4. The American Colonies and Paper Money....... 24
5. Central Banking in the United States.............. 28
6. The Federal Reserve System......................... 49
7. Money Buys the Media................................ 57
8. The Evils of Unsound Money........................ 64
9. The Power of Money to Influence.................. 72
10. Money Manipulation and Legalized Plunder.. 86
11. Banking and the New World Order................ 99
12. Regaining a Sound Perspective..................... 109
13. Restoring the American Dream..................... 129
Notes.. 136
Bibliography... 141
Index.. 144
About the Author... 155

INTRODUCTION

The *American Heritage Dictionary* defines manipulation as, "shrewd or devious management, especially for one's own advantage." For the most part, the secret side of money is a story of manipulation. This manipulation is most often upon the part of politicians and bankers in order to gain possession of others men's wealth, often without their victims being aware of how it happened.

The subject of money, and its manipulation, is of prime importance because sound money is one of the key elements of man's well being. Without sound money human progress toward a better way of life grinds to a halt. In our modern way of life money is the substance that makes everything else possible. It oils the wheels that keep all commerce moving.

In spite of its importance, the subject of money has often been obscured by outright deceit and omission of vital information. Because of this, probably not more than one person in a thousand has more than a limited understanding of the subject. It is our hope that the following pages will greatly increase that understanding.

We give credit to G. Edward Griffin's *The Creature From Jekyll Island: A Second Look at the Federal Reserve* for the inspiration to produce *The Secret Side of Money*. Without the information Mr. Griffin's work supplied, many important elements of the story of money and its manipulation would be missing.

— The Author

THE SECRET SIDE OF MONEY

CHAPTER 1

ANCIENT HISTORY OF MONEY

The history of the use of money goes almost as far back as the recorded history of mankind, at least 4,000 years ago. Some of the first references to money are in Genesis, the first book in Old Testament Scripture. Hebrew words for "money" are used over 100 times in the Old Testament. The first mention of gold occurs in the second chapter of Genesis and the first mention of silver occurs in the 13th chapter. Gold is mentioned in the Old Testament over 330 times and silver is mentioned 264 times.

The first reference to gold and silver as a measurement of wealth was in connection with Abram (Abraham) in Genesis 13:2, "And Abram was very rich in cattle, in silver, and in gold." Many other references show that both metals were used as money. Then, as now, value was determined by weight. The ratio of silver to gold in Bible times was 15 to one. During the early days of the American Republic the value of gold was still approximately fifteen times greater than silver.

When Abraham purchased land to bury his wife Sarah, he paid about 10 pounds of silver for it. This was referred to as, "current money with the merchant" in Genesis 23:16. Abraham's time is generally accepted as about 2000 B.C. This shows that the use of silver as a medium of exchange was wide-spread at this early date. Joseph was sold into slavery for 20 pieces of silver (about 1800 B.C.) in Genesis 37:28. Such Bible references abound proving that precious metals were used as money early in recorded history.

Another reference to the early use of money is recorded in Hammurabi's Code, also dated about 4,000 years ago. This set of written laws dealt with such items relative to money as wages, prices, and interest. Hammurabi's Code, carved in stone in the Babylonian language, is preserved in the Louvre Museum in Paris.

From this early start, gold and silver continued to be used as money for thousands of years. There were several reasons for this. One reason was the beauty of both metals, especially as jewelry. They are durable and can be formed into different sizes and shapes. They are relatively scarce and cannot be produced by any process known to man. Perhaps the most important feature is that both metals have intrinsic value as a commodity and are universally desired. These characteristics make gold and silver an ideal store of wealth, which is what real money is.

All of the mystery about money is removed when we realize that sound money is a commodity serving as a medium of exchange. *The American Heritage Dictionary* defines a commodity as, "An article of trade or commerce that can be transported." The important thing about a commodity is its value. Thus, many commodities such as cattle, grain, tobacco, and even salt have been used as money. The two commodities that have withstood the test of time have been gold and silver. In his book *Age of Inflation,* economist Hans F. Sennholz quotes historian Carl Menger as to the development of the use of money:

> Carl Menger's theory of the nature and origin of money still provides the cornerstone for our knowledge of money. Tracing all monetary phenomena back to the choices and actions of individuals, Menger rejected the doctrines so popular then and now that would make the State the inventor and guardian of money. The origin of money was "entirely natural" as economizing and enterprising men sought to exchange their goods and services for more marketable goods that facilitated exchange for other goods. "Money is not an invention of the state," wrote Menger. "It is not the product of a legislative act. Even the sanction of political authority is not necessary for its existence."[1]

Menger was correct because sound money is nothing more than a commodity. Its value should never be set by anything but the marketplace — it should never be set by government. Gold and silver became the world standard for money simply because they had more of real money's characteristics than any other commodity.

An amazing fact about the use of gold as money is its ability to stabilize purchasing power over a long period.

For example, in Ancient Rome the cost of a finely made toga, belt, and pair of sandals was one ounce of gold. Now, two thousand years later, the cost of a well-made suit, belt and pair of shoes is still one ounce of gold. Throughout the 20th century the average wage in the United States, when measured in ounces of gold, has only increased 1% per year. Even this slight increase has not been the result of a change in the purchasing power of gold, but is a result of improved technology. In his book *The Creature From Jekyll Island: A Second Look at the Federal Reserve* G. Edward Griffin stated, "Long-term price stability is possible only when the money supply is based totally upon the gold supply without government interference."[2]

A forward step in man's economic progress was the minting of precious metal coins. According to Dr. Sennholz, this probably began in Asia Minor in about 650 B.C.:

> To avoid the inconvenience of constant testing and weighing of the metals, the Lydians of Asia Minor in 650 B.C., and soon thereafter the Greeks, began to use coins, which were small pieces of metal with a visible mark of guarantee of weight and fineness. They were manufactured by private and public mints, made of electrum, the natural mixture of gold and silver, and later of bronze, copper, pure gold, and silver, and carried a great variety of symbols and portraits. Coins made of precious metals gradually became the most popular medium of exchange all over the world and constituted universal money until the beginning of the twentieth century.[3]

Ancient History of Money

Some writers believed that coins may have been in use as early as 1100 B.C. When kings began minting coins, the use of coins became even more wide-spread. This also led to abuse by dishonest merchants and many kings. One of the first frauds was known as coin clipping by which a small amount of gold would be shaved off coins and melted down to make new ones. This often became common practice with the king's treasury. The next step in debauchery of the money was for the government to dilute the gold or silver content of the coins it minted.

When the citizens discovered this, they discounted the coins, leading to higher prices. Since each coin was worth less, it took more of them to purchase any item. The goods were not worth more. The coins were worth less. A lesson of history that bankers and politicians move heaven and earth to keep secret, is that whenever prices continue to rise over a long period it can only mean one thing, the money is being debauched. This is just as true today as it was two thousand years ago.

When people try to protect themselves by demanding real money, governments pass legal tender laws to force the acceptance of the debauched money at face value. Anyone who refuses is subject to a fine or imprisonment. In ancient times it could mean death. Governments never have to pass laws to force people to accept sound (commodity) money.

Another thing that always happened when the value of coins was diluted was that real coins disappeared from circulation. When the United States government began issuing coated tokens for silver coins in the 1960s, the solid silver dimes, quarters, and half-dollars went out of circulation. This has always been the case throughout recorded history. It is a sad commentary, but governments have seldom been honest about money. In modern times, politicians and bankers have debauched the money to a degree undreamed of by ancient kings.

An example of the results of government debauchery of money, given by G. Edward Griffin, was the Roman Empire:

> The experience of the Romans was quite different. Basically a militaristic people, they had little patience for the niceties of monetary restraint. Especially in the later Empire, debasement of the coinage became a deliberate state policy. Every imaginable means for plundering the people was devised. In addition to taxation, coins were clipped, reduced, diluted, and plated. Franchises were given to favored groups for state-endorsed monoplies, the origin of our present-day corporation. And, amidst constantly rising prices in terms of constantly expanding money, speculation and dishonesty became rampant.
>
> By the year 301 A.D., mutiny was developing in the army, remote regions were displaying disloyalty, the treasury was empty, agriculture depressed, and trade almost at a standstill. It was then that Diocletian issued his famous price-fixing proclamation as the last measure of a desperate emperor. We are struck by the similarity to such proclamations in our own time. Most of the

chaos can be traced directly to government policy. Yet, the politicians point the accusing finger at everyone else for their "greed" and "disregard for the common good."[4]

Diocletian's answer to the government created crisis was more government in the form of wage and price controls. This resulted in the destruction of the economy and the end of the Roman Empire.

Fortunately, there are also examples of the results of sound money. In Ancient Greece the *drachma* became the most important monetary unit of the civilized world because of the dependability of its gold content. For centuries these coins were the standards by which all others were measured. Sound money enabled the cities of Greece to flourish and its trade to prosper.

The Byzantine Empire is another good example. Constantine established a gold piece called the *solidus*. Its weight was fixed at 65 grains and remained so for eight-hundred years. As a result the Byzantine Empire became the center of world commerce. It never found itself in bankruptcy or even in debt. Not once did it devalue its money. Such a sound money policy enabled Byzantium to control both the civilized and barbarian worlds.

CHAPTER 2

EARLY HISTORY OF BANKING

Banking and coinage began in Early Greece about the same time. At first banks were simply warehouses for the safekeeping of coins, usually silver and gold. Under this arrangement, the depositor was charged a fee for storage and was given a receipt for his money.

Problems began when banks started using their depositors' money for commercial enterprises and to earn interest by lending. To do this they issued more receipts than they had coins in their vaults. This practice led to what became known as fractional-reserve banking. It simply meant that the money reserves were only a fraction of the receipts issued against them. This always led to disaster and bank failure.

Human nature being what it is, the temptation to make ever increasing amounts of profit by lending other people's money was too great to resist. Once it began, there was no point at which it could be reversed. Depositors would eventually discover that there was not enough money in the vaults to cover the receipts, and there was a run on the bank. Those who got there before the bank closed its doors got their money. The rest lost all of their savings. Throughout the history of banking this course of events has been the rule rather than the exception. There were a few good banks that served to show the benefits of sound banking. However, in the end, they too succumbed to the siren call of fractional-reserve banking.

Venice was an important example of sound banking. In 1361, a law was passed by the Venetian Senate that prevented bankers from using depositors' money for their own commercial enterprises. Banks were required to open their books for public inspection and to have their stock pile of gold coins open for viewing. However, they could still lend money.

Eventually, the practice of lending money against reserves led to the failure of the largest bank at that time (Pisano and Tiepolo 1584). Venice then established a state bank that was not allowed to make loans. The bank was limited to charging fees for coin storage, exchanging currencies, handling transfers of payments between customers, and notary service. It was not allowed to lend money or use depositors' money for commercial enterprises.

The bank (*Banco della Piazza del Rialto*) became one of the world's first models of sound banking. Besides maintaining an honest stock of coins to back the receipts it issued, the bank evaluated the true value of each coin it took in and issued a receipt reflecting its true worth. Because of this, public confidence was such that the bank's receipts were accepted widely. Not only were they widely accepted, a premium was paid for the receipts because the public knew that they reflected the true worth of the coins in deposit.

Unfortunately, this example of honest banking was not to last. When the Venetian Senate needed additional revenue, rather than raise taxes, they set up a new bank (*Banco del Giro* 1619) that could create money out of nothing and loan it to the government. The money was created by issuing more receipts than coins to back them. Fractional-reserve banking was again established. Years later the *Banco della Piazza del Rialto* was merged with the new bank and history's first great example of sound banking ended.

G. Edward Griffin had this to say about banking conditions during this period:

> Throughout the fifteenth and sixteenth centuries, banks had been springing up all over Europe. Almost without exception, however, they followed the lucrative practice of lending money which was not truly available for loan. They created excess obligations against their reserves and, as a result, every one of them failed. That is not to say that their owners and directors did not prosper. It merely means that their depositors lost all or a part of their assets entrusted for safekeeping.[1]

The Bank of Amsterdam was another example of sound banking. Founded in 1609, it maintained a policy of strict accountability for about a century. It did not make loans, its income being derived solely from service fees. During this period coins backed all receipts.

Early History of Banking

Since human nature never basically changes, the temptation to gain personal wealth by risking other people's money was too great and the Bank of Amsterdam later began to lend money. When the public finally learned that the bank had lost enormous sums lending money to the Dutch East India Company (in 1790), a steady demand for a return of deposits began. Less than a year later the bank was insolvent and was taken over by the City of Amsterdam.

There was one more example of sound banking. This occurred in Germany with the Bank of Hamburg. For over two centuries it maintained a policy of issuing receipts only for the amount of coins in its vault. The end began when Napoleon took over the bank in 1813. The bank lasted another fifty-five years before it came to an end. With its demise came the end of sound banking throughout the world. From then on all banking was based upon the fractional-reserve system.

The ultimate money manipulation plot in banking was the establishment of a central bank, the first example being the Bank of England. A charter was issued for the formation of the Bank of England in 1694 with the following provisions: (1) The bank would have a monopoly to print paper currency with only a fraction of the amount backed by coin. (2) The bank would then lend the government all the money it needed backed by government I.O.U.s. (3) The government would then pay interest (8%) on this money created out of nothing. (4) The bank could then consider government I.O.U.s as "reserves" upon which to base the creation of more money to lend to private commerce, thus earning more interest on money created out of nothing.

Actually, the term "creating money out of nothing" is a misleading phrase because no one can create money. The newly printed currency only takes on value by decreasing the value of all other paper currency in circulation. This is inflation. What takes place is a transfer of wealth from the people and into the hands of the bankers and politicians who printed the new currency. This is politically safer than raising taxes because very few people understand what is happening.

As always occurs under these circumstances, prices in England began to soar, going up 100% in two years. There was a run on the bank and the Bank of England could not produce coin to back its paper bills. In effect it was bankrupt. Parliament then intervened and a law was passed authorizing the bank to suspend any payment of coin. This kind of maneuver is always called "protecting the public."

In reality the government needed the bank as a cover for pretending to borrow money rather than printing it. The pretence of borrowing served to hide the fact that the government was confiscating the people's wealth through inflation, a hidden tax. As we shall see in a later chapter, the Bank of England was a pattern for the present United States central bank, The Federal Reserve.

CHAPTER 3

THE RISE OF A BANKING DYNASTY

The most important name in the history of banking is that of Rothschild. From a humble and difficult beginning, The House of Rothschild grew into the most powerful banking dynasty on earth. Its establishment took place within the life span of just two generations. Understanding the conditions that made this possible is an important key to understanding how modern day manipulation of money is used to control historical events.

The early ancestors of the Rothschilds settled in Frankfurt, Germany where many members of the Jewish race were attracted because of its trade. Situated near the Rhine, Frankfurt became the gateway for Germany's trade with the western states. Here the Jews were free to operate until a period of harsh oppression began in 1462. This began with the passage of laws restricting the Jews to a section of the city now defined as the ghetto. It was described as a single dark alley, about twelve feet broad, laying between the city wall and a trench.[1]

In his book *The Rise Of The House Of Rothschild* Count Corti described the restrictions placed upon the Jews in Frankfurt:

The Jews were not allowed to acquire land, or to practice farming or handicrafts. They were also forbidden to trade in various commodities, such as fruit, weapons and silk. Moreover, except during fairs, they were forbidden to offer their wares anywhere outside the Jewish quarter. They were forbidden to leave the space within the ghetto walls by night, or on Sundays or holy days. If a Jew crossed a bridge he had to pay a fee for doing so. They were not allowed to visit public taverns and were excluded from the more attractive walks in the city. The Jews accordingly did not stand high in public esteem. When they appeared in public, they were often greeted with shouts of contempt and stones were sometimes thrown at them. Boerne has stated that any street urchin could say to a passing Jew, "Jew, do your duty," and the Jew then had to step aside and take off his hat. However that may be, the oppressed condition of the Jews and the bent of many of them to usury, combined with the natural hostility of the Christians and their feeling that they were not as sharp in business, created an atmosphere of mutual hatred that can scarcely have been more painful anywhere than in Frankfort.[2]

It was into this kind of atmosphere that Meyer Amschel Rothschild was born in 1743. By the time he was ten years old, Meyer Amschel was employed by his father in the business of money-changing. This involved exchanging gold and silver coins for copper known as coarse money. Money-changing, a profitable business at that time, was a necessity for those traveling any distance because of the many different systems of currency throughout Germany. This experience led Meyer Amschel to become a dealer in rare coins. At the age of twelve, Meyer lost both of his parents. Left with a small inheritance, he continued the family business, showing amazing ability for his age.

Meyer was educated in the Jewish faith at Fürth. After that he joined the firm of Oppenheim at Hanover. Here he gained additional knowledge of business and met Hanoverian General von Estorff who employed him to obtain valuable coins for his collection. Meyer's association with General Estorff not only fired his zeal for numismatics, it also provided a valuable business connection.

It was through General von Estorff that Meyer was introduced to William, Prince of Hanau who was also a collector of rare coins. Because of his business relations with William, Meyer later acquired the title of "Crown Agent to the Principality of Hesse-Hanau." This title was a key that would open many doors for the House of Rothschild.

At the age of 27, Meyer's assets were such that he could consider marriage and a family. On August 29, 1770 he married the daughter of a tradesman named Wolf Solomon Schnasser. To this union were born five daughters and five sons. The five sons Amschel, Solomon, Nathan, Carl Meyer, and James all grew up working in the family business; and eventually became partners with their father.

Meyer's growing prosperity enabled him to move his family into a larger house that, in comparison to many Jewish homes of the time, was a fine home. By modern standards it was scarcely livable for a family of twelve. On the ground floor it had two small rooms, one for the parents and one for all the children. The kitchen was five by twelve with a small hearth and a bench. A primitive pump conveyed water to the kitchen. This was considered a great luxury for the time. A narrow staircase led to the maid's small room on the second floor. A small passage led to a tiny roof terrace. Behind the house was a room about nine feet square. This room was the first banking house of the Rothschilds. The Rothschild's house was still standing as late as 1927.

Besides their natural talents for business, there were varied circumstances that enabled the House of Rothschild to rise to the position of one of the great international bankers of the world. One of these was the everlasting tendency of governments to spend beyond their means and make up the difference by borrowing money. Once the Rothschilds accumulated enough capital to make sizable loans, heads of states beat a path to their door. This was often for personal loans as well as loans for the public treasury.

The major factors were, however, the tremendous events that took place at the time and the hidden forces behind these events. The Rothschilds have been described as "the right people, in the right place, at the right time." A brief but enlightening explanation of these forces was given in the publishers introduction to Count Corti's book *The Rise Of The House Of Rothschild:*

> The period of years covered by The Rise Of The House Of Rothschild, 1770-1830, is one of the most important but also one of the most misunderstood eras in Western history. During this period emerged a conspiratorial force which not only plunged France, and Europe, into chaos, nihilism, slaughter and tyranny, but which is still so active that it has become the dominant factor in the political, financial, and even religious events of the world today. This Conspiracy was founded on May 1, 1776, by Adam Weishaupt, a professor at the University of Ingelstadt, and called the Order of the Illuminati. Its stated purpose was, and is, to destroy all governments, nations, and religions and to erect on the ruins of civilization a New World Order ruled by the Illuminati.[3]

These events were described at the time of the French Revolution by Francis of Austria:

> [N]ot only every territorial prince and government of whatever kind they may be, but also every private person possessed of any property, or who has been blessed by God with any possessions or rights acquired by inheritance or otherwise must realize with ever growing conviction . . . that the war is a universal war declared upon all states, all forms of government, and even upon all forms of private property, and any orderly regulation of human society, as is clearly proved by the chaotic condition and internal desolation of France and her

raging determination to spread similar conditions throughout the world.[4]

As we shall see in our progress through history, these events would have a profound effect upon the money systems of the world right up to the present day. The part the Rothschilds played in this was also briefly explained in the publisher's introduction to Corti's book:

> . . . the chaos the Conspiracy (the Illuminati) unleashed on Europe obliterated many of the vital foundations of Western Civilization. Yet it also provided tremendous opportunities for those who could turn the events of the time to their advantage, and such were the Rothschilds. And they repaid the Conspiracy, at first perhaps unwittingly, by building a financial structure which greatly altered, to the Conspiracy's advantage, the traditional monetary relations of state with state and which helped to guarantee the elimination of the stabilizing influence of the nobility from positions of economic and political power. [5]

The wars throughout Europe that followed the French Revolution gave the Rothschilds opportunity to reap great profits in the financial and trading business associated with war requirements. These profits formed the real foundation of the enormous fortune built up by the Rothschilds. When Napoleon declared a blockade against English commerce and communications, smuggling became an exceedingly profitable operation for the

Rothschilds; for, by this time the family was already engaged in extensive trade by land and sea, flying its own flag on its own ships.

When France became in dire need of English goods, Napoleon permitted a form of officially sanctioned smuggling for certain items. Special custom locations were set up where approved contraband could be imported. Through this avenue flowed money, goods, and correspondence. So efficient were their methods that the Rothschilds were even able to ship large amounts of gold through France to Wellington in time of war. This enabled Wellington to maintain his army in Portugal and in the Pyrenees mountains between Spain and France. Without this aid he may not have been able to defeat Napoleon at Waterloo.

The Rothschilds not only controlled their own means of shipping, they also established an elaborate system of communications. Their ability to carry documents and letters was so good that it was sometimes chosen above that of the official post. This may have afforded another advantage for the family as it made it possible to open important mail to learn early news of coming events. Financial decisions could then be made based on this information.

The Rothschild's system of communication was honed to perfection, even surpassing that of the military. When Napoleon was defeated by Wellington at Waterloo, Nathan Rothschild received the news in London by his carrier in the early hours of June 20. This was twenty-four hours before Wellington's courier, Major Henry Percy, arrived.

When the London stock exchange opened the next morning, Nathan was on hand. All eyes were on Nathan when, with a dejected look, he began to sell his holdings. As a result the market panicked. Knowing that the Rothschilds usually had advance information, Nathan's selling signaled to all present that Wellington had lost and prices would tumble. The market dropped in wave after wave until it hit bottom. At that point Nathan reversed his call and purchased the entire market of government bonds. By this action he had acquired the dominant holding of England's entire debt. Later when a member of the Rothschild family tried to get a court order to suppress a book containing this information, the court ruled that the information was true and dismissed the suit.

Eventually the five brothers settled in five different locations establishing family headquarters in Vienna, Frankfurt, Paris, London, and Naples. Along the road to fame and fortune, Meyer and his sons met and conducted business with many of the most powerful people in the world. During fifteen years of war in Europe they conducted some risky business and encountered many dangerous situations. At one point Napoleon shelled Frankfurt resulting in the destruction of several houses in the Jewish quarters. The Rothschilds' house only suffered minor damage.

After defeating Prussia, Napoleon decided to remove William of Hesse who was now one of the richest men in Europe. When William was forced to flee, he hid much of his treasure with one most important chest of securities being entrusted to the Rothschilds. Napoleon sent agents to search the Rothschilds' house, but they had been forewarned and had hidden the chest in their basement. When the agents demanded to see the business records, they were shown a second set of books with no record of their dealings with William. Throughout the war, they carried on extensive business with William. This often required long and dangerous trips by coach for Meyer Rothschild. During this time the Rothschilds also conducted extensive business with Metternich who was at the time the most powerful man in Europe.

A most interesting association was that of the Rothschilds with Marie Louise, wife of Napoleon I and daughter of Francis. Marie Louise was described by Corti as "calloused and pleasure-loving," and "living only for her own amusement."[6] She had stayed with Napoleon as long as he was successful. When he fell from power, she took her son and returned to her father without shedding a tear for Napoleon. She never visited him in exile or even bothered answering his letters. It was the Rothschilds who helped arrange a trust for her children by Count von Neipperg.

In time, the Rothschilds became prominent international bankers. This distinction put them in a different category from ordinary bankers. In his book *None Dare*

The Secret Side of Money

Call It Conspiracy Gary Allen referred to Dr. Quigley's definition of international bankers:

> In describing the characteristics of the Rothschilds and other major international bankers, Dr. Quigley tells us that they remained different from ordinary bankers in several ways: they were cosmopolitan and international; they were close to governments and were particularly concerned with government debts, including foreign government debts; these bankers came to be called "international bankers."[7]

More important than the interest made on money lent to governments was the influence bankers had over the debtor nations. Gary Allen explained it this way:

> You can control a government if you have it in your debt; a creditor is in a position to demand the privileges of monopoly from the sovereign. Money-seeking governments have granted monopolies in state banking, natural resources, oil concessions and transportation. However, the monopoly which the international financiers most covet is control over a nation's money.
> Eventually these international bankers actually owned as private corporations the central banks of the various European nations. The Bank of England, Bank of France and Bank of Germany were not owned by their respective governments, as almost everyone imagines, but were privately owned monopolies granted by the heads of state, usually in return for loans. Under this system, observed Reginald McKenna, President of the Midlands Bank of England: "Those that create and issue the money and credit direct the policies of government

Rise of a Banking Dynasty

and hold in their hands the destiny of the people." Once the government is in debt to the bankers it is at their mercy. A frightening example was cited by the *London Financial Times* of September 26, 1921, which revealed that even at that time: "Half a dozen men at the top of the Big Five Banks, could upset the whole fabric of government finance by refraining from renewing Treasury Bills."[8]

It is very important to note that the central banking mechanism set up in Europe was a monopoly able to create money out of nothing and loan it to governments for interest. It could be called the most successful method of banking robbery (robbery by the bank) in the world. For in this case, not only was the wealth of the people confiscated through the process of inflation, they were also taxed to pay the interest on nothing more than a bookkeeping entry. The method of secretly confiscating wealth through inflation, as used by central banks past and present, is morally wrong. The method is more important than the names of the people involved because it amounts to a form of legalized theft that is carried on from generation to generation.

CHAPTER 4

THE AMERICAN COLONIES AND PAPER MONEY

Fiat money is essentially counterfeit money. It has no intrinsic value nor does it represent anything of intrinsic value such as silver or gold. It has to be forced upon the people by legal-tender laws, making it illegal to refuse it. One of the first records of the wide spread use of fiat money was recorded by Marco Polo in his travels to China during the thirteenth century.

Here the Emperor's mint in the City of Cambaluc would make up something resembling sheets of paper from white skins found between the wood and outer bark of certain trees. These sheets would be cut into different sizes representing different values and colored black. Then they were adorned with official signatures and seals. Last they were stamped with the Emperor's seal. The people throughout the kingdom were then forced to use these pieces of paper as money. The penalty for refusal was death. In this manner the emperor could confiscate any amount of the wealth of the people he desired.

The next outstanding example of the use of fiat money was in the American colonies. In his book *The*

The American Colonies and Paper Money

Creature From Jekyll Island: A Second Look at the Federal Reserve G. Edward Griffin explained how this came about:

> The first colonial experience with fiat money was in the period from 1690 to 1764. Massachusetts was the first to use it as a means of financing its military raids against the French colony in Quebec. The other colonies were quick to follow suit and, within a few years, were engaging in a virtual orgy of printing "bills of credit." There was no central bank involved. The process was simple and direct, as was the reasoning behind it. As one colonial legislator explained it: "Do you think, gentlemen, that I will consent to load my constituents with taxes when we can send to our printer and get a wagon load of money, one quire of which will pay for the whole?"
>
> The consequences of this enlightened statesmanship were classic. Prices skyrocketed, legal tender laws were enacted to *force* the colonists to accept the worthless paper, and the common man endured great personal losses and hardship. By the late 1750s, Connecticut had price inflated by 800%, the Carolinas had inflated 900%, Massachusetts 1000%, Rhode Island 2300%.[1]

The hardest hit were those who trusted the government, some losing everything they had. Those who were more cautious came out much better.

When the war with England started in 1775, the money supply was about $12 million. By the end of five years it had been inflated to $650 million. This was an expansion of the money supply 5,000%. The value of the

Continental (the colonial monetary unit) dropped from one dollar in gold in 1775 to twenty-five cents in 1778. By 1779 it was worth less than a penny and ceased to circulate. This resulted in the saying "Not worth a Continental." At this time shoes cost $5,000 a pair and a suit of clothes cost a million dollars.

When the people tried to prevent the loss of their savings by raising prices and demanding gold for payment, as always, wage and price controls and legal tender laws were passed. The forcing of fiat paper money upon the people brought great loss and hardship to the colonists leading to conditions approaching anarchy. G. Edward Griffin explained the seriousness of the situation:

> All of this was painfully fresh in the memories of the delegates to the Constitutional Convention and, as the opening session convened in Philadelphia in 1787, there were angry mobs in the streets threatening the legislators. Looting was rampant. Businesses were bankrupt. Drunkenness and lawlessness were everywhere to be seen. The fruit of fiat money had ripened, and the delegates did not enjoy its taste.
>
> In October of 1785, George Washington wrote: "The wheels of government are clogged, and... we are descending into the vale of confusion and darkness." A year later, in a letter to James Madison, he said: "No day was ever more clouded than the present. We are fast verging to anarchy."
>
> In February of 1787, Washington wrote to Henry Knox: "If any person had told me that there would have been such formidable rebellion as exists, I would have thought him fit for a madhouse."[2]

The reason the authors of the Constitution rejected paper money, and only authorized the government to "coin" money, was that they had witnessed first hand the bitter fruits of governments issuing fiat money. Had the Founding Fathers not been wise enough to demand a sound monetary system backed by gold and silver, the young Republic probably would not have survived. The phrase in the Constitution copied from the Articles of Confederation that allowed the government to "emit bills of credit" (print fiat money) was removed by a vote of over four to one.

CHAPTER 5

CENTRAL BANKING IN THE UNITED STATES

The first central bank in the United States was the Bank of North America. It was chartered by the Continental Congress in the Spring of 1781, seven years before the Constitution was ratified. It was modeled after the Bank of England and allowed to issue paper promissory notes in excess of the amount of gold and silver backing them. Although it could not directly issue the nation's money, it was granted a monopoly in its field. It was also the official depository for federal funds. One of its first acts was to create $1.2 million and loan it to the government.

The bank was organized by a member of Congress, Robert Morris, who was a wealthy Philadelphia merchant. It was a fraudulent operation from the very beginning. When Morris couldn't raise the $400,000 from private investors, as required by the charter, he resorted to devious means. He arranged to have gold, lent to the United States by France, deposited in the bank. He then used this as a fractional-reserve base to create enough money to lend to himself and his associates for the subscription. The bank was short lived. Congress did not renew its charter and the bank did not survive beyond the end of the war.

The Articles of Confederation permitted the government to "issue bills of credit" (print money), but when the Constitution was written that permission was removed. Unfortunately, the government was still granted the power to borrow money. This was the loophole that enabled the politicians to circumvent the Constitution and create a central bank with the power to create money out of nothing and lend it to the government. In this manner the government wasn't printing money, the bank was.

In reality the bank was not lending money to the government, it was creating money for the government by inflating the money supply. This was a way to silently confiscate the wealth of the people by the unseen tax of inflation. The people were not only robbed of their wealth by inflation of the money supply; they were also taxed to pay the interest on money created out of nothing and lent to the government. This amounted to an infinite amount of interest because there is no way to put a percentage of interest on money created out of nothing.

The second central bank in the United States was the First Bank of the United States. Alexander Hamilton, then Secretary of the Treasury, proposed its creation in 1790. It is surprising that Hamilton would propose the creation of a central bank as he had been a strong proponent of sound money during the Constitutional Convention.

Thomas Jefferson strongly opposed Hamilton on this issue. This division led to the creation of our first political parties. It was a debate that was to be waged in Congress for decades. Jefferson argued that the Constitution did not authorize Congress to create a bank, and that allowing a bank to create money could only lead to national ruin. Jefferson stated, "A private central bank issuing public currency is a greater menace to the liberties of the people than a standing army."[1]

Hamilton argued that debt, if limited, was good. He also argued that, although the Constitution did not directly grant Congress the power to create a bank, it expressed that power as a necessity in order to carry out the functions expressly granted to government. Hamilton stated, "No society could succeed which did not unite the interest and credit of rich individuals with those of the state."[2] This is of course exactly what a central bank does. The problem is that it always works to impoverish the common people and further enrich the elite who control the bank.

Hamilton won, and in 1791 Congress granted a twenty-year charter to the First Bank of the United States. It was also modeled after the Bank of England and was a carbon copy of the previous Bank of North America. The bank had a monopoly to issue bank notes that were legal tender for all debts to government in the form of taxes and duties. It was required to redeem its notes in gold or silver; however, since it was a fractional-

Central Banking in the United States

reserve bank, it could issue more notes than it had gold or silver with which to redeem them.

The president of the bank was Thomas Willing who had also been involved with Robert Morris in the Bank of North America. Thomas Willing had been a member of the Continental Congress and was one of those who voted against the Declaration of Independence. Again, federal funds were used to make up the lack of private capital required by the charter. The bank opened with less than nine per cent of the $10 million legally required.

In *The Creature From Jekyll Island* G. Edward Griffin quotes three noted authors on the Rothschild involvement in the Bank of the United States:

> Who were these private investors? Their names do not appear in the published literature, but we can be certain they included the Congressmen and Senators—and their associates—who engineered the charter. But there is an interesting line in Galbraith's text that hints at another dimension to the composition of this group. On page 72 of *Money: Whence It Came, Where It Went*, he states matter-of-factly: "Foreigners could own shares but not vote them." What a story is hidden behind that innocuous statement. The blunt reality is that the Rothschild banking dynasty in Europe was the dominant force, both financially and politically, in the formation of the Bank of the United States. Biographer, Derek Wilson, explains: "Over the years since N.M. [Rothschild], the Manchester textile manufacturer, had bought cotton from the Southern states, Rothschilds had

developed heavy American commitments. Nathan ... had made loans to various states of the Union, had been, for a time, the official European banker for the US government and was a pledged supporter of the Bank of the United States."

Gustavus Myers, in his *History of the Great American Fortunes*, is more pointed. He says: "Under the surface, the Rothschilds long had a powerful influence in dictating American financial laws. The law records show that they were the power in the old Bank of the United States." The Rothschilds, therefore, were not merely investors nor even an important power. They were *the* power behind the Bank of the United States![3]

As with previous central banks, the main purpose of the First Bank of the United States was to create money for the federal government. In the next five years the bank created $6.2 million for the government. As a result, prices went up 72% during that period. This means that 42% of the value of the people's money was confiscated by the government through the hidden tax of inflation. However, the hidden tax was not equal. It had far less impact upon the wealthy and did not hinder the elite who engineered the bank from reaping huge profits.

Public opinion began to turn against the bank with the main opposition coming from two factions. One was the Jeffersonians who wanted sound money backed by gold and silver. The other faction was made up of small bankers, land speculators, and industrialists who wanted to be free to create as much unbacked money as they could get away with. At the time there were a large

Central Banking in the United States

number of banks known as "Wildcat Banks" because they were in such remote locations that they were said to have only wildcats for customers. These banks wanted to be free from even the limited restrictions placed upon them by the First Bank of the United States. After a heated battle, the bill for the renewal of the charter of the First Bank of the United States was defeated in the House by one vote and in the Senate by one vote. This ended the second central bank in the United States, but the worst was yet to come.

The next great robbery of the American people by the bankers and politicians came during the War of 1812. To finance this unpopular war, the government encouraged an enormous expansion in the number of state banks. These banks then printed huge amounts of notes to buy government bonds. The government then used this money to purchase war materials.

The state banks tripled the money supply causing the dollar to shrink to about one-third of its former purchasing power. When the depositors began to demand their gold instead of paper, the banks closed their doors. Passions ran so high that the banks had to hire guards to protect their officials and employees from the angry mobs wanting their money. This time sixty-six per cent of all the money held during that period had been confiscated from the American people through the instrument of inflation.

At this time a new dimension was also added to the partnership between bankers and politicians. The politicians decided to protect the bankers from their contractual obligations by allowing them to stay in business while refusing to redeem their notes in gold or silver. This set a precedent for all such future financial crises.

One of the most tragic lessons of history is that men seldom learn from history. This is especially true when it comes to matters of money and banking. The history of the third central bank established in the United States was a repeat of the history of the previous two central banks. Every mistake of the past was repeated, with Congress being herded like sheep by the bankers.

Congress granted the Second Bank of the United States a twenty-year charter in 1816. Again, it was a carbon copy of the previous bank; but this time some new dimensions were to come into play that would greatly affect the future of America. To begin with, Congress received $1.5 million for granting the charter. This could rightly be called a bribe. As the previous bank, it only raised $2.5 million of the $7 million required by the charter with the largest block of stock being held by foreign investors.

During this time state banks also proliferated, growing in number by 46% in two years. As a result, the money supply was expanded by $27.4 million. This caused a loss of 40% of the value of the people's money due to inflation.

One of the new dimensions added to banking during this period was the creation of boom-bust cycles. This

Central Banking in the United States

was accomplished by first expanding then contracting the money supply. When the bank caused a depression in 1818 by contracting the money supply it was justified on the grounds of slowing down inflation, a problem caused by the bank in the first place. The power to expand and contract the nation's money has been used as a political weapon ever since. Under a sound gold-and-silver backed monetary system, America would never have seen the endless boom-bust periods that have resulted in the people being repeatedly sheared like sheep. Under a free enterprise system, with sound money, there will always be adjustments caused by a free market; but overall, there will be a steady, gradual climb in prosperity. There would be no severe boom-bust cycles such as are always the result of a central banking system with the power to expand and contract the money supply.

As the country sank into severe depression because of the central bank's contraction of the money supply, a storm of controversy arose. The two leading opponents were President Andrew Jackson and Nicholas Biddle, president of the Bank of the United States. The battle came to a head just as President Jackson was coming up for reelection. Biddle took advantage of the moment to request Congress to renew the bank's charter, thinking that Jackson would not be anxious to stir up too much controversy while running for reelection. He was able to get the Republicans to back the bill and Congress to pass it, but he had failed to reckon with the determination of Andrew Jackson. Jackson vetoed the bill.

G. Edward Griffin explained the event in this manner:

> It was brilliant strategy on Biddle's part but it didn't work. Jackson decided to place his entire political career on the line for this one issue and, with perhaps the most passionate message ever delivered to Congress by any President, before or since, he vetoed the measure. The President's biographer, Robert Remini, says: "The veto message hit the nation like a tornado. For it not only cited constitutional arguments against recharter—supposedly the only reason for resorting to a veto—but political, social, economic, and nationalistic reasons as well." Jackson devoted most of his veto message to three general topics: (1) the injustice that is inherent in granting a government-sponsored monopoly to the Bank; (2) the unconstitutionality of the Bank even if it were not unjust; and (3) the danger to the country in having the Bank heavily dominated by foreign investors.
>
> Regarding the injustice of a government-sponsored monopoly, he pointed out that the stock of the Bank was owned only by the richest citizens of the country and that, since the sale of stock was limited to a chosen few with political influence, the common man, not only is unfairly excluded from an opportunity to participate, but he is forced to pay for his banking services far more than they are worth. Unearned profits are bad enough when they are taken from one class of citizens and given to another, but it is even worse when the people receiving those benefits are not even citizens at all but are, in fact *foreigners*. Jackson said: "It is not our own citizens only who are to receive the bounty of our Government. More than eight millions of the stock of this bank are held by foreigners. By this act the American Republic proposes virtually to make them a present of some millions of

dollars.... It appears that more than a fourth part of the stock is held by foreigners and the residue is held by a few hundred of our own citizens, chiefly of the richest class. For their benefit does this act exclude the whole American people from competition in the purchase of this monopoly and dispose of it for many millions less than it is worth."[4]

Jackson was a powerful adversary, but Biddle still had an ace in the hole; and that was his control over Congress. This had, of course, been accomplished with money. An outstanding example was Daniel Webster who had been an advocate of sound money in Congress until he went on Biddle's payroll. From then on he campaigned for the bank. When he represented the bank before the Supreme Court (*McCullock v. Maryland*), it was Webster's twisted logic that caused the Court to circumvent the Constitution and help to destroy sound money. Webster also made public speeches in defense of the bank. In these speeches he implied that the bank was a defender of sound gold-and-silver backed money when in reality it was just the opposite. Such is the power of money to corrupt even the greatest of men.

Congress, the banks, speculators, industrialists, and segments of the press were behind the bank. Jackson made his appeal to the people. Describing the bank as a "hydra-headed monster" his position was "Bank and no Jackson, or no bank and Jackson!" Jackson won fifty-five per cent of the popular vote and eighty per cent of the vote in the electoral college, the vote in the electoral college being the most significant. This was a safeguard put in the Constitution by the Founding Fathers to divide the power of government. The members of the electoral college were chosen by the states and had the responsibility of electing a president based on merit. Another safeguard put in the Constitution was the election of Senators by state legislators. The Senators were to represent the states. The people had the responsibility of electing the members of The House of Representatives to represent them.

The President's first action after being reelected was to direct the Secretary of the Treasury to remove all federal deposits from the Bank of the United States. The Secretary, William Duane, refused and was told that his services would no longer be required. Beginning on October 1, 1833 federal deposits began to be withdrawn from the bank.

An enraged Biddle chose to use his power to manipulate the money system of the United States to force Congress to counter Jackson's move by plunging the nation into a depression. Biddle's arrogance and disregard for the American people were revealed by Remini:

> Biddle counterattacked. He initiated a general curtailment of loans throughout the entire banking system.... It marked the beginning of a bone-crushing struggle between a powerful financier and a determined and equally powerful politician. Biddle understood what he was about. He knew that if he brought enough pressure and

agony to the money market, only then could he force the President to restore the deposits. He almost gloated. "This worthy President thinks that because he has scalped Indians and imprisoned Judges, he is to have his way with the Bank. He is mistaken." "The ties of party allegiance can only be broken," he declared, "by the actual conviction of existing distress in the community." And such distress, of course, would eventually put everything to rights. "Nothing but widespread suffering will produce any effect on Congress.... Our only safety is in pursuing a steady course of firm restriction—and I have no doubt that such a course will ultimately lead to restoration of the currency and the recharter of the Bank.... My own course is decided. All other banks and all the merchants may break, but the Bank of the United States shall not break."[5]

Biddle's contraction of the money supply resulted in a severe depression. When Congress reconvened in December, the nation was in an uproar. All the blame was directed toward the President for his action against the bank. For the first time in American history, the Senate voted to censure the president. The turning point came when Governor George Wolf of Pennsylvania publicly denounced the bank and Biddle. Biddle had been so confident that he publicly boasted that he had caused the depression.

A resolution was passed in the House (134 to 82) declaring that the Bank of the United States "ought not to be rechartered." A resolution was also passed calling for a Congressional investigation into the bank's involvement in causing the depression. When Biddle refused to cooperate with Congress in the investigation, the sun began to set on his career.

For the first time in history, an assassination attempt was made on a president of the United States. The would be assassin, Richard Laurence, got off on a plea of insanity. Later he told a friend that he had been in contact with European bankers who promised to come to his aid if he got caught. This was one of those amazing events in history when man proposes, but God disposes. Andrew Jackson's life was spared because both of Lawrence's pistols had failed to fire.

As to Biddle's career, the bank charter expired in 1836 and the bank was restructured as a state bank. After a spree of speculation, lavish advances to bank officers, and suspension of payment in specie (coins), Biddle was arrested and charged with fraud. He was undergoing civil litigation when he died. Within five years the bank closed its doors.

By 1836 Jackson had slain the "hydra-headed monster;" however, its offsprings were still alive in the form of Jackson's enemies. The Administration pushed a series of monetary reforms through Congress aimed at restoring the use of gold and silver as everyday money. Banks were limited to issuing notes only above five dollars. This was later increased to twenty dollars. This required the use of coins for small transactions and limited bank notes to use in larger commercial exchanges. The move failed to accomplish its purpose because the increased

Central Banking in the United States

use of check book money made the use of coins unnecessary. The reforms were eventually dismantled by Congress.

Amazing as it is, politicians have been willing to try every means to establish a sound monetary system except a fully gold-and-silver backed currency. No matter how often fractional-reserve banking had failed, it was always resurrected. Once hooked, the politicians could not resist the temptation to use the hidden tax of inflation.

Different methods were devised to try to avoid the consequences of fractional-reserve banking. In New England the creation of money was based on a ratio of bank assets. Banks could only create two hundred per cent of their assets in gold or silver. This held up fairly well until check book money came into use. While there was a limit on the amount of bank notes that could be issued in relation to gold and silver deposits, there was no limit on the amount of check book money that could be created. As a result, thirty-two Massachusetts banks closed between 1837 and 1844. The money lost was the gold and silver deposited by the people with a solemn promise that it could be redeemed any time. It was not the bank's to lend out.

Another method invented to allow banks to create money out of nothing without consequences was the creation of a safety net to bail out the banks that got into trouble. First established in New York in 1829, the law required each bank to contribute a certain amount of its capital each year until it reached three per cent. This went into a fund to rescue banks that could not meet their commitments. Since all banks had to pay into the fund, all of them eventually began to rely on it and to take greater chances. This led to the draining of the fund, and it was later abandoned. A similar fund was tried in Michigan in 1836 but it lasted less than a year.

One method tried was to base the creation of money on government securities, meaning government debt. It was tried in the 1850s by: Illinois, Indiana, Wisconsin, and other Midwestern states. This led to an endless chain of debt creation and inflation until the panic of 1857 brought it to a close.

Another proposal for creating money with nothing more than a bookkeeping entry was to back it with state credit. In 1835 Alabama created a state bank funded by a public bond issue of $13,800,000. Paper money became abundant creating a false aura of prosperity that was short lived. When it came to an end in the panic of 1837, the people who had lent their real money to the venture lost almost all of their investment plus what they lost through inflation.

Mississippi created a state bank in 1838 by issuing $15,000,000 in government bonds as backing for its notes (paper money). The bank folded within four years and the bank repudiated its obligations on the bonds. As a result, $48,000,000 of the bank's loans were never paid, and $23,000,000 of its notes and deposits were never redeemed. The economic devastation caused so many people to flee the state that it gave rise to the saying — "G.T.T." gone to Texas.

Money based upon the full faith and credit of the state was also tried in Illinois, Kentucky, Florida, Tennessee, and Louisiana. All these attempts failed. Arkansas tried making real estate the basis of creating money. This also failed. All of these banking disasters could have been avoided if the government had simply created really free-banking by enforcing banking contracts the same as all other contracts and then staying out of the banking business.

The Civil War was another period of massive inflation. Contrary to popular myth, the cause of the war was not the issue of slavery. Even after the war had started in 1861, Lincoln made it plain that the reason for the war was not the issue of slavery:

> My paramount object in this struggle is to save the Union, and it is not either to save or destroy slavery. If I could save the Union without freeing any slave, I would do it; and if I could save it by freeing all the slaves, I would do it; and if I could do it by freeing some and leaving others alone, I would also do that.[6]

Lincoln was personally opposed to slavery but he also realized that it was being gradually abolished throughout the civilized world and in time would end in America without bloodshed. Many in the South felt the same way. The Emancipation Proclamation was a desperate move by Lincoln to get support for the North and to neutralize its enemies in England and France. Lincoln explained this himself:

> Things had gone from bad to worse until I felt we had reached the end of our rope on the plan we were pursuing; that we had about played our last card, and must change our tactics or lose the game. I now determined upon the adoption of the emancipation policy.[7]

There were several reasons for the conflict outside the issue of slavery not the least of which was the involvement of European bankers. G. Edward Griffin quoted the observations of German Chancellor Otto von Bismarck:

> The division of the United States into federations of equal force was decided long before the Civil War by the high financial powers of Europe. These bankers were afraid that the United States, if they remained in one block and as one nation, would attain economic and financial independence, which would upset their financial domination over the world. The voice of the Rothschilds prevailed. They saw tremendous booty if they could substitute two feeble democracies, burdened with debt to the financiers,... in place of the vigorous Republic sufficient unto herself. Therefore, they sent their emissaries into the field to exploit the question of slavery and to open an abyss between the two sections of the Union.[8]

The observations of Bismarck were probably correct. At the time the Rothschilds had extensive commercial and financial dealings in the United States. Their agent, August Belmont, had placed large amounts of Rothschild money into the bonds of state supported banks in the South. In the North, Belmont was the chief agent for the sale of Union bonds in England and France. He was also an associate of George Sanders, an American who was a leader in a European revolutionary organization called Young America.

A direct successor to Young America was an organization called The Knights of the Golden Circle. This organization, headed by George Bickley, became an underground army numbering in the hundreds of thousands. Bickley became head of the Secret Service in the South. The Knights of the Golden Circle was a secret organization dedicated to revolution and conquest. The plan of its leaders was to carve out an empire with Cuba as the center of a circle that reached from Panama to Pennsylvania. This resulted in the name Knights of the Golden Circle. It had ties to a branch of the Illminati in France called the Seasons.

Two famous names associated with the Knights of the Golden Circle were Jesse James and John Wilkes Booth. That Booth was a member of the K.G.S. was proven by Booth's granddaughter, Izola Forrester, years after the assassination of Lincoln. Many documents relating to the time were discovered by Izola and related in her book *This One Mad Act*. This evidence was found when government documents were declassified in the 1930s and pointed to a cover up of the involvement of the K.G.C. in the Lincoln assassination.

Economic conflict was the main issue that led to secession and the beginning of the war. This began when Congress passed laws levying stiff import duties on items coming from Europe that were also manufactured in the North. The main product of the South, cotton, was not protected from European competition. Because of the import duties, Europeans stopped buying American cotton and the South had to pay higher prices for Northern goods. This resulted in great economic hardship for the South. Pressure from the North about slavery added to the tensions, finally resulting in secession and war. There is reason to believe that all of this was promoted by powerful international forces for their own gain in wealth and power.

To finance the war, in 1862 the Union Treasury began printing huge amounts of paper bills, eventually adding up to $432 million. These were known as greenbacks because they were printed with green ink. These were legal-tender for debts, public and private, but not for government duties or taxes.

In 1863 Congress passed the National Banking Act establishing a system of nationally-charted banks with the purpose of raising money for government military expenses. This was accomplished by the banks purchasing government bonds that were traded back to the government for United States Bank Notes that were legal tender for taxes and duties. These notes circulated as

Central Banking in the United States

money and were lent out for interest. Although the banks traded in their government bonds for United States Bank Notes, they still collected interest on the bonds. Thus, they made double interest. The banks were only required to keep twelve per cent of the value of the bank notes they issued in silver and gold. This means that eighty-eight per cent of the notes had no backing whatever. This system was the beginning of creating money out of government debt and the beginning of perpetual debt for the United States. The economic consequences of the creation of paper money during the war resulted in the people in the North surrendering half of all the money they earned during that period. Taxes were in addition to this amount. The South created about a billion dollars in paper money. This resulted in prices rising by 9,100%. With the defeat of the South, all of its paper currency became worthless. G. Edward Griffin gave this information about the system:

> As usual, the average citizen did not understand that the newly created money represented a hidden tax which he would soon have to pay in the form of higher prices. Voters in the Northern states certainly would not have tolerated an open and honest tax increase of that magnitude. Even in the South where the cause was perceived as one of self defense, it is possible that they would not have done so had they known in advance the true dimension of the assessment. But especially in the North, because they did not understand the secret science of money, Americans not only paid the hidden tax but applauded Congress for creating it.

On June 25, 1863, exactly four months after the National Bank Act was signed into law, a confidential communique was sent from the Rothschild investment house in London to an associate banking firm in New York. It contained an amazingly frank and boastful summary: "The few who understand the system [bank loans earning interest and also serving as money] will either be so interested in its profits or so dependent upon its favors that there will be no opposition from that class while, on the other hand, the great body of people, mentally incapable of comprehending,... will bear its burdens without complaint."[9]

Griffin's summary of this dark period in America's history is as follows:

America's bloodiest and most devastating war was fought, not over the issue of freedom versus slavery, but because of clashing economic interests. At the heart of this conflict were questions of legalized plunder, banking monopolies, and even European territorial expansion into Latin America. The boot print of the Rothschild formula is unmistakable across the graves of American soldiers on both sides.[10]

CHAPTER 6

THE FEDERAL RESERVE SYSTEM

In 1913 the Federal Reserve became the fourth central bank in the United States. The name "Federal Reserve" was chosen to hide the fact that it was a private bank by implying that it was federal. The word "reserve" was thrown in to make it sound even better. It was created by Congress with the passage of the Glass-Owen Bill on December 22, 1913. Since then the Federal Reserve Act has been amended 195 times to make it what it is today, a private bank with monopoly power to control the money system of the United States. Although the visible heads of the System, the members of the Federal Reserve Board, are appointed by the President and confirmed by the Senate, they answer to no one for their decision making. The bank has never been audited nor does anyone outside its inner circle know who the real powers are behind the scene.

Much of the groundwork to sell the American people on the idea of the Federal Reserve System was done by Paul Moritz Warburg, a European Banker. Warburg was a leading member of the banking firm of M.M. Warburg and company of Hamburg Germany, and Amsterdam, the Netherlands. He and his brother Felix came to the United States and, with Rothschild money, purchased a partnership in Kuhn, Loeb and Company. There is some indication of the ideological slant of this company in that Jacob Schiff, head of the New York based Kuhn, Loeb and Company, spent $20 million to help bring about the Bolshevik revolution in Russia. Warburg became one of the wealthiest men in America, obtaining domination over the country's railway system. Because of his wealth and power, he became the inspiration for the character Daddy Warbucks in the comic strip *Little Orphan Annie*.

Paul Warburg had a third brother, Max Warburg, who became the director of the *Reichsbank* in Germany. It was a central bank, and was used as one of the models of the Federal Reserve. It was the *Reichsbank* that created the massive inflation that ruined the German economy and set the stage for Hitler to come to power.

The meeting in which the Federal Reserve System was formulated was held in absolute secrecy in the private hunting lodge of J.P. Morgan. The lodge was located just off the coast of Georgia on Jekyll Island. The participants had departed at night from the New Jersey railway station in the private railway car of Senator Nelson Aldrich. All members were instructed to arrive at the railway station separately and to only use their first names to conceal their identity. Although the meeting was kept secret, and denied for many years, it was later confirmed by several writers, two of whom were Paul Warburg and Frank Vandelip. Both of these men were present at the meeting.

Another participant, Nelson Aldrich, a United States Senator from Rhode Island, was an investment associate of J.P. Morgan and had extensive holdings in banking, manufacturing, and public utilities. He was also the father-in-law of John D. Rockefeller, Jr. Other members in this elite group were: Abraham Piatt Andrew, Assistant Secretary of the United States Treasury; Frank A. Vanderlip, president of the National City Bank of New York, a Rockefeller bank with ties to Kuhn, Loeb & Company; Henry P. Davison, senior partner of the J.P. Morgan Company; Charles D. Norton, president of J.P. Morgan's First National Bank of New York; and Benjamin Strong, head of J.P. Morgan's Bankers Trust company. At the time (1910) these seven men represented an estimated one-fourth of the entire wealth of the world.

Publicly these men represented the Morgan group and the Rockefeller group which were at the center of control over financial resources in the United States. Privately they had strong ties to the Rothschild group. Paul Warburg was a representative of the Rothschilds with close banking ties in Europe. Connections between the Morgans and Rothschilds went back to the days of George Peabody, J.P. Morgan's mentor.

In 1848 Alphonse Rothschild came to the United states and, after an extended visit, recommended that a Rothschild House be established in America. It is possible that the Morgan operation was a front for the Rothschild consortium in America. Such suspicions were aroused when J.P. Morgan, Sr. died in 1913 leaving an estate far lower in value than would be expected for one who controlled so much wealth. This was also the case when Jack Morgan died in 1943. However, whatever the extent of Rothschild influence in the creation of the Federal Reserve System, the attitude of the men who met on Jekyll Island to formulate the bank was European — it was not American.

Selling the Federal Reserve scheme to the American people and getting Congress to pass legislation creating it was a classic example of duplicity upon the part of politicians and bankers. After the first attempt to pass the Federal Reserve Act (the Aldrich Bill) failed, a new strategy was developed. With minor changes the Bill was labeled as banking reform. In order to get support for their so-called banking reform, the money powers set about to get their man in the White House. The man they selected was Woodrow Wilson.

William Howard Taft (Republican), who was now up for reelection, had fallen into disfavor with big business and the bankers because he had refused to back the Aldrich Bill. In order to defeat Taft and elect Wilson, the money powers backed Teddy Roosevelt whose candidacy split the Republicans and pulled votes away from Taft. Publicly, Wilson and Roosevelt went around the country preaching against the evils of the money trust. Privately they were both committed to promoting the interests of the system they were denouncing. The

The Federal Reserve System

scheme worked, and Wilson won with 42 percent of the popular vote.

In addition to J. P. Morgan, another of the main powers behind Wilson was Edward Mandel House. A socialist, House would later found the Council on Foreign Relations (C.F.R.), an organization created to so change America that it would give up its sovereignty and accept world government. House was such a dominant force over Wilson that he even lived in the White House part of the time. House became the chief negotiator between the money powers and Wilson, his greatest effort being to get the Federal Reserve Act passed.

To fool the American people into believing that the Bill was really banking reform, while privately working for its passage behind the scenes, the bankers made a public show of opposing it. The turning point came when William Jennings Bryan, then the most influential Democrat in Congress, was convinced to support the Bill. His turnabout came after he was awarded the position of Secretary of State.

Operating as a cartel with control over the banking system in America, the Federal Reserve has presided over one of the largest hidden transfers of wealth in the history of mankind. Since its inception, at least 90% of the value of the U.S. dollar has been transferred into the hands of the bankers and politicians through the mechanism of inflation.

The monetary system has been changed to the point that all gold and silver backing has been removed from the currency, and we now have only pure fiat money with nothing but debt to back it. Under the system as it exists today, all money is created by debt. The money you deposit in the bank can be used to generate up to nine times its value in debt. Thus, if you deposit one thousand dollars, the bank can generate up to eight thousand dollars in loans. This debt is the only asset backing your deposit.

Money is created through nothing more than a bookkeeping entry and loaned to the public for interest. A young couple buying a home today pays twice as much money for interest than it does for the house itself. Thus the price of a home is tripled because of interest paid on money created out of nothing. To make matters worse, the home owner is further penalized by loss of buying power because of the inflation caused by creating money out of nothing.

The creation of the Federal Reserve also gave the money manipulators the power to yo-yo the economy by expanding and contracting the money supply. A prime example of this was the great depression of 1929. From 1921 to 1929 the money supply was increased by 61.8%. Stock prices soared, credit was easy, loans were cheap, and paper profits high. Even the banks became speculators.

After a private meeting in February 1929 between Montagu Norman of the Bank of England and the officers of the Federal Reserve, leading Wall Street figures began getting out of the stock market. While this

The Federal Reserve System

was going on, the public was being assured that all was well and the existence of the Federal Reserve was a safeguard against calamity. On October 29 the crash began in earnest. Within twelve months $40 billion vanished. The stocks that had been sold for a fraction of their worth were then purchased back by the Wall Street giants who had been forewarned of coming events. The son-in-law of Roosevelt, Curtis Dall, labeled this as, "...calculated shearing of the public by the World-Money powers."[1]

Today it is possible for the Federal Reserve to monetize the debt of the entire world and lay the burden of payment upon the backs of the American tax payers. This is how it works. When the Federal Reserve makes a loan to a foreign country such as Mexico or Russia, the loan is considered an asset. Based on this I.O.U., money is created out of thin air by a bookkeeping entry. The resulting inflation (expansion of the money supply) is then paid for by the American people in reduced buying power. If the borrower can't, or won't, repay the loan the United States Government guarantees payment, which of course means American taxpayers. This makes it possible for the taxpayers to pay for the loan twice, once by inflation, and once by taxation. The bankers risk nothing.

One of the worst effects of the Federal Reserve System has been to lock the nation into perpetual debt by making debt the only backing for the entire money supply. If all debts public and private were repaid, all of the money would disappear back into the ink wells and computer systems from which it was created. On the other hand, the greater the debt, the greater the money supply. The greater the money supply the greater the inflation. The greater the inflation, the greater the transfer of wealth into the hands of the bankers and politicians. By this system the American people are slowly being reduced to poverty as the wealth flows into the hands of the money manipulators at the top.

While establishing this system, the bankers made sure that they were protected. If some members of the banking cartel got into trouble, a bailout system was provided whereby a member could go to the Federal Reserve and borrow enough to recover. This money also comes from the taxpayers through inflation. If conditions get bad enough, the taxpayers are forced to pay for the losses directly through taxation.

Most of the politicians in Congress go along with these schemes because they use the Federal Reserve as a means of channeling money into their hands without the people understanding what is happening. The reason that Karl Marx called for the creation of a central bank in the Communist Manifesto is that a central bank is the one sure means of establishing socialism in an industrialized nation. With a central bank socialism is inevitable. Without a central bank socialism is impossible. Our central bank, the Federal Reserve, makes it possible for the American free enterprise system to be replaced by socialism. It must be abolished.

CHAPTER 7

MONEY BUYS THE MEDIA

Knowing that it would take tremendous propaganda to convince the public to accept their schemes, early in the 20th century the money manipulators decided to buy up control of the opinion-molding media in the United States. This was an important move on their part because it also gave them the power effectively to censor their opposition. The following article stating how this was accomplished was inserted in the Congressional Record in 1917 by Congressman Oscar Callaway:

> In March, 1915, the J. P. Morgan interests, the steel, shipbuilding, and powder interests, and their subsidiary organizations, got together 12 men high up in the newspaper world and employed them to select the most influential newspapers in the United States and sufficient number of them to control generally the policy of the daily press of the United States.
> These 12 men worked the problem out by selecting 179 newspapers, and then began, by an elimination process, to retain only those necessary for the purpose of controlling the general policy of the daily press throughout the country. They found it was only necessary to purchase the control of 25 of the greatest papers. The 25 papers were agreed upon; emissaries were sent to purchase the policy, national and

The Secret Side of Money

international, of these papers; an agreement was reached; the policy of the papers was bought, to be paid for by the month; an editor was furnished for each paper to properly supervise and edit information regarding the questions of preparedness, militarism, financial policies, and other things of national and international nature considered vital to the interests of the purchasers. . . . This policy also included the suppression of everything in opposition to the wishes of the interests served.[1]

The *New York Times* had already been purchased by Alfred Ochs in 1896, with financial help from J.P. Morgan, Rothschild agent August Belmont, and Jacob Schiff of Kuhn, Loeb & Co. With this kind of backing, the *Times* was sure to support the views of the New York bankers. Those who later took over the paper became members of the CFR, as also did a number of their reporters. Herbert L. Matthews of the *Times* was a strong supporter of Castro's takeover of Cuba. Mathews was a CFR member.

Another newspaper with strong CFR influence is the *Washington Post*. It was purchased in 1933 by Eugene Meyer, a Federal Reserve board governor, who joined the CFR in 1929. When he took over the *Post*, one of the first things he did was fire the editor because he refused to support the government's recognition of the Soviet Union. Meyer's daughter, Katharine Graham (CFR), later took over the paper. Some of its top people are CFR members. The *Post* also owns *Newsweek* magazine. Its editor-in-chief and editor are also CFR members.

Money Buys the Media

Time magazine was founded by CFR member Henry Luce who was aided in his career with loans from several CFR friends who had ties to Morgan banking. Time Inc. has several CFR members on its board of directors. It publishes *People, Life, Fortune, Money,* and *Sports Illustrated* magazines.

The major TV networks are also under CFR influence. William Paley who was chairman of the board of CBS for years was CFR. Chairman Thomas H. Wyman was CFR. In 1987, eleven out of fourteen board members were CFR. Dan Rather of CBS is a CFR member.

NBC is a subsidiary of RCA which was headed by David Sarnoff, a CFR member. Chairman Thornton Bradshaw and several board members are also CFR. Tom Brokaw of NBC is also a CFR member.

ABC has CFR members on its board and in its news department. Two of these are CFR member Ted Koppel and CFR member David Brinkley.

What all of this means for the American people is that the information they receive from the major newspapers, magazines, and television is filtered to present a certain point of view. For decades that viewpoint had been a reflection of the socialistic, anti-American bias of the money manipulators who control the media.

Nor does the problem end with control over the major media. After WWII the money powers decided to extend their domination to include the book publishing and distribution industry. This was done to prevent a repeat of the kind of criticism of the events of WWI that was published after the end of the war. Historian Charles Beard explained this in a *Saturday Evening Post* article in 1947:

> The Rockefeller Foundation and Council on Foreign Relations . . . intend to prevent, if they can, a repetition of what they call in the vernacular "the debunking journalistic campaign following World War I." Translated into precise English, this means that the foundation and the council do not want journalists or any other persons to examine too closely and criticize too freely the official propaganda and official statements relative to "our basic aims and activities" during World War II. In short, they hope that, among other things, the policies and measures of Franklin D. Roosevelt will escape in coming years the critical analysis, evaluation and exposition that befell the policies and measures of President Woodrow Wilson and the Entente Allies after World War I.[2]

In 1953, Harry Elmer Barnes explained how this policy actually worked:

> The methods followed by the various groups interested in blacking out the truth about world affairs since 1932 are numerous and ingenious, but, aside from subterranean persecution of individuals, they fall mainly into the following patterns or categories: (1) excluding scholars suspected of revisionist views from access to public documents which are freely opened to "court historians" and other apologists for the foreign policy of President Roosevelt; (2) intimidating publishers of books

Money Buys the Media

and periodicals, so that even those who might wish to publish books and articles setting forth the revisionist point of view do not dare to do so; (3) ignoring or obscuring published material which embodies revisionist facts and arguments; and (4) smearing revisionist authors and their books. . . .

As a matter of fact, only two small publishing houses in the United States — the Henry Regnery Company and the Devin-Adair Company — have shown any consistent willingness to publish books which frankly aim to tell the truth with respect to the causes and issues of the second World War. Leading members of two of the largest publishing houses in the country have told me that, whatever their personal wishes in the circumstances, they would not feel it ethical to endanger their business and the property rights of their stockholders by publishing critical books relative to American foreign policy since 1933. And there is good reason for this hesitancy. The book clubs and the main sales outlets for books are controlled by powerful pressure groups which are opposed to truth on such matters. These outlets not only refuse to market critical books in this field but also threaten to boycott other books by those publishers who defy their blackout ultimatum.[3]

What was stated by Barnes over 40 years ago is essentially true today. It has changed somewhat due to the advent of desk top publishing and the growth of the self publishing industry. However, in order to distribute their books, small publishers, in most cases, must create their own markets.

Education also became a victim to the money powers. This was made possible by the establishment of the large tax-free foundations near the beginning of the 20th century. These were established before the graduated income tax so that the super rich could retain control of their wealth and use it to their own discretion without paying income tax. This placed them at a tremendous advantage over the rest of the population in controlling the major institutions in the United States.

In the early 1950s a committee of Congress was established to investigate these foundations. This was known as the Reece Committee in recognition of its chairman Carrol Reece of Tennessee. The staff director of the committee was Norman Dodd. In the process of their investigation, the committee discovered that the minutes (1908) of the Carnegie Endowment for International Peace recorded a discussion about the effectiveness of using war to alter civilization. In 1909 the Carnegie leaders discussed how to get the United States into a war, which came to pass under the Wilson administration. This was World War I.

In a 1982 videotaped interview, Norman Dodd explained how the interests of the Carnegie trustees shifted to education after the end of the war:

> At that time their interest shifts over to preventing what they call a reversion of life in the United States to what it was prior to 1914, when World War I broke out. And they, at that point, come to the conclusion that to prevent a reversion, we must control education in the United States. And they realize that that's a pretty big task. To them it's too big for them alone, so they

approach the Rockefeller Foundation with a suggestion that: That portion of education which could be considered domestic be handled by the Rockefeller Foundation, and that portion which is international could be handled by the endowment, and they then decide that the key to the success of these two operations lay in the alteration of the teaching of American History.

So they approach four of the then most prominent teachers of American History in the country — people like Charles and Mary Beard, and their suggestion to them is that they alter the manner in which they present this subject, and they got turned down flat. So they then decide that it is necessary for them to do as they say "build our own stable of historians." And then they approach the Guggenheim Foundation, which specializes in fellowships and say, "When we find young men in the process of studying for doctorates in the field of American History and we feel that they are the right caliber, will you grant them fellowships on our say-so.?" And the answer is "Yes." So under that condition eventually they assemble twenty. And they take this twenty potential teachers of American History to London, and there they are briefed as to what is expected of them, when as, and if they secure appointments in keeping with the doctorates they will have earned. That group of twenty historians ultimately becomes a nucleus of the American Historical Association.[4]

Subversive forces were so strong that the Reece Committee was not able to finish its investigation and bring this information to the American people.

CHAPTER 8

THE EVILS OF UNSOUND MONEY

One of the evils of unsound money is its deception. All of its effects work toward destruction while on the surface they appear to be for good. This has been well understood by those who have worked for world wide revolution. In his book *Financial Terrorism,* John F. McManus quoted the world famous British socialist John Maynard Keynes as to how inflation of the currency can affect a nation:

> Lenin is said to have declared that the best way to destroy the Capitalist System was to debauch the currency. By a continuing process of inflation, governments can confiscate, secretly and unobserved, an important part of the wealth of their citizens. By this method they not only confiscate, but they confiscate arbitrarily; and, while the process impoverishes many, it actually enriches some. The sight of this arbitrary rearrangement of riches strikes not only at security, but at confidence in the equity of the existing distribution of wealth. Those to whom the system brings windfalls... become "profiteers," who are the object of hatred of... [those] whom the inflationism has impoverished.... As inflation proceeds... the process of wealth-getting degenerates into a gamble and a lottery.

The Evils of Unsound Money

Lenin was certainly right. There is no subtler, no surer means of overturning the existing basis of society than to debauch the currency. This process engages all of the hidden forces of economic law on the side of destruction, and does it in a manner which not one man in a million is able to diagnose....[1]

Keynes and Lenin knew the effects of debauching money because they knew the history of money, something the majority of the American people have not been allowed to learn. An article in *American Opinion* magazine quoted author Donald J. Hoppe as to the results of Roman money being totally debased:

> [T]he Roman Emperors caused inflation by "coin clipping," debasing the coin of the realm to pay their debts. The silver *antoninius* originally contained eighty-four grains of the precious metal, but in only fifty years had been reduced to a thinly silver-plated slug ....
> By the end of the third century A.D., Roman money had been totally debased, and Donald J. Hoppe writes as follows: "...What gold and silver were left rapidly fled beyond the borders of the Empire. Price controls and legal tender laws were passed in profusion, to no avail. The decline of Rome and the decline of its money went hand in hand. Rioting and lawlessness, dishonesty and corruption were aggravated by the spectacle of emperors and governments that were little more than liars and embezzlers themselves.
> At last, with its treasury empty, its farms rotting in neglect, industry stagnant and mired in financial disorder, trade reduced to almost a barter level and a frantic speculation devouring the last vestige of organized

commercial activity, the mightiest empire the world had ever seen drifted helplessly into barbarism. It never recovered from the monetary madness of the third century. Long before the Huns and Vandals set foot within its boundaries, the Roman Empire committed suicide by monetary debasement and inflation."[2]

This is exactly what has been happening in the United States since the creation of the Federal Reserve. At least 90% of the value of the dollar has been taken out of the hands of the majority of the people and placed in the hands of a few, resulting in all of the attending evils forecast by Lenin and Keynes. The reason that Karl Marx called for the creation of a national bank with monopoly power over a nation's money system is that inflation is one of the main tools that make revolutions possible. One of the reasons the Communists boast that socialism is inevitable, is that a central bank makes it inevitable. Without a central bank, socialism is impossible. The United States is following in the footsteps of Rome; and unless our direction is reversed, we will reap the same disastrous consequences.

The *American Opinion* also gave several examples of debauching of the money resulting in revolution:

> The conspirators behind the French Revolution again purposely destroyed the currency with deficit in the 1790s, pumping out 35 billion *assignats*, and it bankrupted the workingman and was used to justify rationing and terror. Communists taking control in Russia and China did the same thing, forcing people to

The Evils of Unsound Money

sell their homes for bread. In the 1920s Germany was similarly victimized through its equivalent of the Federal Reserve, which to meet deficits was printing 46 billion new marks a day. Soon a single U.S. dollar was worth billions of marks, and men had to be paid three times a week in huge baskets. The economic chaos was followed by Hitler's National Socialism.[3]

As also stated by Keynes, inflation is indeed a process that very few people understand. This is true simply because the truth about the cause of inflation has been obscured by leading economists and politicians. An outstanding example was the program launched by President Gerald Ford called "Whip Inflation Now" (WIN). The people of the nation were told that in order to cure the problem of inflation they had to sacrifice, wear things out, make due with what they had, stop wasting food, plant gardens, and wear WIN buttons, all of which had absolutely nothing to do with increasing the money supply. Thus, the blame was shifted to the public when politicians and bankers were responsible for creating the problem. Another ploy used by economists who are in on the game is to pretend that no one really understands what causes inflation.

Lenin and Keynes also understood that the inflationary process created class hatred and was destructive to a sound sense of values and morality. This has worked in America with the level of unsound money coinciding with the low level of morality. One reason for this is that the massive transfer of wealth caused by inflation places the bulk of the money into the hands of those working for less than honorable goals. In this case, a few decide who receives support for their endeavors. The vast majority of the people who labored to create the wealth are left with little or no say in such matters.

In his book *Age of Inflation* Hans F. Sennholz made this comment about inflation:

> Inflation destroys individual thrift and self-reliance as it gradually erodes personal savings. As it benefits debtors at the expense of creditors, it creates a massive flow of unearned income and loss. It consumes productive capital and destroys the middle class that invests in monetary instruments. It generates the business cycle, the stop-and-go, boom-and-bust movements of business that hurt millions of people. It invites government price and wage controls and other restrictive policies that hamper individual freedom and activity. In short, inflation breeds economic upheaval and social disorder, and generally erodes the moral and social fabric of a free society.[4]

The destruction of morality is one of the greatest benefits to the manipulators who wish to rule over their fellow man. The creation of large sums of money that have not been earned by the production of goods or services become a powerful tool to corrupt. As history shows, not even religion is always a successful barrier to its influence. Scripture confirms this view in I Timothy 6:10, "For the love of money is the root of all evil: which while some coveted after, they have erred from the faith, and pierced themselves through with many sorrows." All seven of the major translations of Scripture in use today make it plain that some gave up their faith in pursuit of money.

One of the greatest moral philosophies of all time is that veracity is the heart and core of morality. The word "veracity" is defined by *The American Heritage Dictionary* as, "Habitual adherence to the truth." Honesty and truth are synonyms for the word veracity. To rationalize away the importance of this is to strike a blow against one of the main pillars of society. Yet, dishonesty in money manners is not only practiced by governments; it is also practiced by religious leaders. This is especially true when an unsound monetary system of inflated fiat money is prevalent.

An outstanding example is that of religious leaders who tell their followers that the way to get is to give; and that if they will send them a gift (always money) God will multiply their gift and return it many fold. Scripture is often quoted to back up this appeal.

The hypocrisy of this approach is, that if the fund raisers had indeed discovered the secret of abundance, they would never need to appeal for money. They would simply follow their own advice, go to the bank, draw out their money, and give it away. A greater amount would then return, next day or next month, and they would have more money in the bank than before. The process could be repeated until sufficient was on hand for any need. Obviously, this doesn't work. Neither is the fund raiser confident enough to offer a money back guarantee whereby if a one thousand-dollar gift did not give a larger return, the gift would be returned.

The truth of the matter is, that the honest way to get, is to produce goods or services to exchange to one's fellow man for their goods or services. Anything more than this is an appeal to greed. Prominent religious leaders who have fallen into dishonest practices in money matters have sometimes become the subjects of national disgrace. Even well known charitable and religious organizations have lost hundreds of thousands of dollars by falling victim to an appeal to greed by clever con artists. This is far more prevalent in a society corrupted by an unsound monetary system of fiat money than it is in a sound monetary system.

When the Foundation for New Era Philanthropy filed for bankruptcy on May 15, 1995, it was revealed that as many as 120 Christian organizations had been lured into something like a pyramid scheme by promises of huge returns in a short period. The first investors were paid off with money from new investors until no new investors could be found and the scheme collapsed. Christian organizations had invested more that $100 million dollars in New Era.

The Foundation for New Era Philanthropy was founded in 1989 by John G. Bennett. Bennett promised a 100 per cent return on investments within months because he had anonymous donors who would match the funds of others investors. He later admitted there had never been any anonymous donors.

Bennett operated what is known as a Ponzi scheme. It is named after Charles Ponzi, who in 1920 raised millions of dollars by promising investors 50 percent interest for the use of their funds for forty-five days. Such schemes only last as long as new investors can be found to invest funds which are used to pay off new investors.

Among some prominent organizations involved with New Era were Spring Arbor College, Focus on the Family, and the Christian Broadcasting Network. Even the Boy Scouts of America were taken in. This is not to say that honest fund raising is morally wrong. It is dishonesty and appealing to greed that is wrong.

Another disastrous appeal of inflated amounts of fiat money is that it creates a condition whereby many people can become millionaires. Greed sets in and they strive to use whatever means that works to enrich themselves. What they do not realize is that becoming a millionaire will be of no benefit when a suit of clothes costs a million dollars.

CHAPTER 9

THE POWER OF MONEY TO INFLUENCE

As we have seen, a central bank with the power to confiscate wealth by means of inflation of the money system has access to vast amounts of money taken from the people who earned it. As history shows, this system has always been operated as a partnership between bankers and politicians, which of course means government. This money can then be used to mold ideals, values, and actions in the direction desired by the power brokers. Mighty forces can be directed simply by channeling vast sums of money into the right hands. This is most often proclaimed for the public good, but is often just the opposite and usually results in more government.

An outstanding example of this began with a public announcement at a press conference by scientist Robert Gallo on April 23, 1984. This event was sponsored by Margaret Heckler, Secretary of Health and Human Services who introduced Gallo to the press corps. The news was earthshaking. Gallo announced that he had discovered the virus that caused the infectious plague known as AIDS. From that time on every federal dollar spent on AIDS research was spent only from the viewpoint that Gallo's HIV virus caused AIDS. The amount

The Power of Money to Influence

of money spent would eventually add up to billions of dollars.

From the very beginning there were some questionable things about this whole business. One was that the virus had actually been first discovered by French scientist, Luc Montagnier. Gallo had also departed from the ethical protocol among scientists requiring that he first publish papers on his discovery for review by his fellow scientists before going to the news media. This departure from ethics was all the more suspicious because Gallo had a track record of being involved in false claims. In 1992 he was officially convicted on a charge of scientific misconduct by The Office of Research Integrity. Gallo appealed the decision, some rules were changed, and he was acquitted. Gallo later secured the U.S. patent rights for the virus test, which meant a profit for him whenever the tests were used.

The news of the discovery of a deadly contagious virus panicked the public. The government had to do something. Congress opened the treasury, and billions started flowing. These billions were channeled through the Center for Disease Control (CDC) and used to establish one of the most gigantic medical bureaucracies of all time. The CDC AIDS education program influenced virtually every avenue of public opinion including the Red Cross, public schools, political organizations, medical organizations, Gay Rights groups, and even the Religious Right. CDC AIDS education material even went to 23,000 Christian bookstores in the U.S. The major news media was naturally the main objective.

Millions of dollars flowed freely to thousands of scientists by way of grants to study the AIDS plague. An inoculation against the HIV virus had to be found before it was too late. Dire predictions were daily put forth. Surgeon General C. Everett Koop and the World Health Organization were predicting 100 million people would be infected by early 1990 as it exploded into the heterosexual population. Since HIV was a blood-borne virus perhaps even a mosquito could spread AIDS. Fifty to 100 percent of everyone carrying the virus would die. A war on AIDS must be declared!

To carry on this war effectively it would be necessary greatly to increase the power of government. In his book *Why We Will Never Win The War On AIDS*, Byran J. Ellison quoted the following plans called for by Donald Francis:

> Referring directly to the mandate provided by *Confronting* AIDS, Francis called for five major steps to expand CDC authority. First, he wanted the CDC to receive a special status, making it immune from accountability to the voters. "The United States needs to establish a separate line of public health authority that allows for accountability, yet is protected from extremist interference. Perhaps the Federal Reserve is an example to emulate... Specific legislation should be promulgated to protect CDC from political interference with necessary public health practice."

Second, he proposed "guaranteed health care" for HIV positives, mostly to lure infected people out of hiding. "If we are going to be successful in identifying HIV-infected persons through testing programs," he said, "the necessary incentive must be guaranteed health care financing."

His third point called for endorsing drug use, using the logic that providing drugs to addicts would prevent sharing of dirty needles. "Following a more enlightened model for drug treatment, including prescribing heroin, would have dramatic effects on HIV and could eliminate many of the dangerous illegal activities surrounding drugs." Francis even called this "safe injection." But if heroin itself causes AIDS, then taxpayers would be financing the deaths of addicts.

Fourth, he advocated heavier federal intervention in producing vaccines, apparently ignoring the lessons of the 1976 disaster with the swine flu vaccine.

Finally, Francis issued a call to consolidate public health authority in central hands. "Establish clear chains of responsibility," he insisted. "CDC needs to reestablish its leadership role in HIV prevention. Prevention requires close coordination, training, and financial support of state and local health departments." This would subject all public health functions in the country to CDC control.[1]

It is generally unknown to the American public that the collectivists who wish to control the human race strive for government control of medicine as an important part of their program. Socialized medicine forced upon the people by compulsory government programs was used by Bismarck in Germany as far back as 1884.

Lenin taught that socialized medicine was a keystone in the arch of the socialist state. It began in the Soviet Union in the early 1930s.

In 1919 a world wide socialist organization was formed which worked to establish socialized medicine throughout the world. This organization was known as the International Labor Organization (ILO) and was part of the Treaty of Versailles resulting from the Paris Peace Conference. The United States became a member of the ILO in 1934 under the Roosevelt administration. A drive for socialized medicine, led by the Social Security Department, then began in this country.

Since then, the collectivists have made great progress toward establishing total government control over medicine. A medical crisis, real or imagined, would most likely be used to justify much greater government control over medicine and all the details of human life connected with it. This should make the questionable aspects of the AIDS crisis of concern to every freedom loving American.

In the haste to find a cure for the AIDS virus a toxic drug known as AZT was hurriedly approved for AIDS treatment in 1989, and later approved for AIDS prevention in 1990. First developed as a treatment for cancer, AZT was shelved because of its severe toxic side effects, one of which was the destruction of the immune system. At first there was a reaction against the use of the drug by several leaders in the homosexual

The Power of Money to Influence

community, its use being strongly denounced in many of their publications.

In order to silence these objections, the manufacturers of AZT started financing their opponents by placing expensive ads for the drug in the homosexual publications and contributing large sums of money to homosexual activists groups. The power of money won the battle and those who opposed the use of AZT got on the bandwagon.

Meanwhile, back at the laboratory, there were a few scientists who were raising some serious questions about the HIV hypothesis. How could HIV (a retrovirus) cause a breakdown in the immune system when retroviruses have never been known to inhibit or kill rapidly dividing cells? Except for correlation, the existence of HIV in AIDS victims, there had been no scientific experiments to prove that HIV causes AIDS. There were also cases of AIDS victims who were HIV negative. In July of 1992 *Newsweek* reported several such cases. In fact, the test for HIV finds only the antibody to HIV, not the virus itself. In addition, out of one million people in America reported to be HIV positive, only 300,000 developed AIDS. And how could a virus be so selective as to pick male homosexual drug users as 90% of these victims?

To be proven scientifically a hypothesis must be demonstrated repeatedly in the laboratory without a single exception. In the case of HIV, the time-tested rules of Koch's postulates were never used to validate the claim that HIV was the cause of AIDS. One of Koch's rules to prove a microbe the cause of a disease is that the microbe must be found in all cases of the disease. HIV fails this test. Also the microbe must be isolated from the host and grown in pure culture. This can be done with the HIV virus but only with great difficulty because it is only found in humans in a latent form and must be reactivated with powerful chemical stimulants. In order to be the proven cause of a disease, the microbe must also reproduce the original disease when introduced into a susceptible host. HIV also fails this test.

One outstanding scientist who questioned the HIV hypothesis was Peter H. Duesberg, a professor of Molecular and Cell Biology at the University of California, Berkeley. Because of his decades of research of viruses, he was elected to the National Academy of Sciences, and received an Outstanding Investigator Grant from the National Institutes of Health (NIH).

In a public speech to the United Republicans of California (UROC) on April 21, 1990, Dr. Duesberg made these comments:

> AIDS is generally described to us as an infectious disease, or one that occurs under bizarre conditions. Bizarre compared to other infectious diseases that you are aware of, in fact, that you may have suffered from. It is bizarre for an infectious disease to occur ten years after infection. We are told when you pick up the Aids virus today, by some form of contact or infusion, by being born to a mother who was infected, your chances of developing Aids are 10 years later. That is you have

The Power of Money to Influence

10 years time to live together with that presumably deadly virus, and not have any symptoms at all.
This is very bizarre in view of everything we have learned in the two thousand years of research on microbes and bacteria. That is if you pick up syphilis today, by some way or another, then you know a month or two later whether you have picked it up and whether you are going to have the disease or not. The same is true for measles, and smallpox, and mumps and hepatitis, and any other infectious disease. Not for this one [AIDS]. Another very peculiar property about this virus is, if it were indeed the cause of it, that AIDS occurs at least in this country and in Europe almost exclusively, that is to 90%, in two risk groups only. And those are either interveinous confirmed drug users or a small percentage, and I emphasize that specifically, a small percentage of male homosexuals. Those are the major risk groups that ever get AIDS. And there is no precedent for a virus or a microbe being that selective, or that picky.
Now I will introduce you today to an alternative view, which suggests that AIDS in fact is not an infectious disease, not one caused by a virus, but is instead a noninfectious condition acquired mostly in this country, and in Europe by drug consumption. That includes legal, psyhco-active drugs, and also some drugs [AZT] that are used to prevent or treat AIDS.[2]

Dr. Duesberg then went on to explain the deadly effect of AZT on all living cells:

That drug [AZT] is for us molecular biologists, a chain terminator of DNA Synthesis. It is a molecule that

79

stops all DNA, that is the genetic material, in all of us living on this planet, that is incorporated into a living cell. So all cells whether it's a plant, a virus, bacterial, or us will die when treated with AZT.[3]

The answer to men like Dr. Duesberg came not in the form of scientific proof but in the form of censorship and financial reprisals. Among major network shows that canceled scheduled interviews with Dr. Duesberg were Good Morning America, Cable News Network, and The Larry King Live program. Scientific journals that had published papers by Duesberg began to turn them down. Major magazines and newspapers killed articles commissioned by themselves. The power of money came into play and Duesberg's funding for research was discontinued.

So, how does the evidence stack up after more than a decade of the AIDS epidemic and 22 billion dollars of taxpayers' money being spent. Bryan Ellison summed it up this way:

> AIDS research has likewise turned embarrassingly futile. The promises of a vaccine and a therapy remain unfulfilled. Public health officials cannot demonstrate they have saved any lives by controlling the blood supply, nor through their programs for promoting and distributing condoms and sterile injection needles. Worst of all, none of the virus-based predictions has been borne out: AIDS has not exploded into the heterosexual population, as do all other sexually-transmitted diseases, nor can doctors predict the course of illness in any given

The Power of Money to Influence

patient, which can involve any combination of some thirty unrelated diseases. And in contrast to the official prediction that HIV would kill virtually all infected people, some two-thirds of the HIV positives have remained AIDS-free for nearly a decade. AIDS officials can neither control nor predict the epidemic, leaving AZT therapy as their only consistent answer—a drug originally developed for cancer chemotherapy that efficiently destroys the immune system and causes symptoms largely indistinguishable from AIDS itself.

As the pinnacle of power in biomedical research, microbe hunting typifies the collapse of true science since World War II. On the surface, this seems incredible. Modern American science was designed to be the best ever, and it now carries that reputation around the world. How could it have gone so wrong, and yet create the illusion of glorious success?

The answer lies in the money. Simply put, science has grown vastly too large, employing far too many researchers generating overwhelming amounts of data. Daniel S. Greenberg, editor of the widely respected newsletter *Science & Government Report*, has referred to biomedical science as "one of the most swollen, overindulged, underexamined, and self-pitying public enterprises on the national landscape."[4]

And how goes the battle for truth after all of this? The good news is that time is always on the side of truth and the tide is changing. In 1991 Charles Thomas, a Harvard University professor, removed himself from the government-funded academic setting, moved to San Diego, California and formed the Group for the Scientific Reappraisal of the HIV/AIDS Hypothesis. By 1994 over four hundred people had joined this organization, most of them scientists and doctors.

Peter Duesberg is now being invited to lecture at some prestigious scientific meetings. He is also being invited to speak at American universities, hospitals and medical centers. His invitations also include conferences in foreign countries. Publishing invitations are being extended to him from many leading scientific journals.

In the September 20, 1993 edition of *The New American* magazine Robert W. Lee stated:

> Following a decade of scientific investigation, a "cure" for acquired immune deficiency syndrome (AIDS) is nowhere in sight. AIDS researchers now say that a vaccine for the human immunodeficiency virus (HIV) may not be available before the year 2000, if then. In fact, there is increasing evidence that the AIDS Establishment's claim that HIV alone causes AIDS may be erroneous. Many factors other than HIV are capable, either by themselves or possibly in conjunction with HIV, of ravaging the human immune system.[5]

It may just be that the end result will be the exposure of the greatest money-manufactured medical crisis in human history.

Another example of the power of money to influence can be illustrated by the example of a national organization that began in 1970. Its advertised purpose was to be a "people's lobby" to represent common folks against "special interests." The organization, Common Cause,

The Power of Money to Influence

had as its chairman John W. Gardner. Following is one of Gardner's statements in his promotion book *In Common Cause*:

> The most serious obstacle the citizen faces when he sets out to participate is that someone with a lot of money got there first and bought up the public address system. The full-throated voice of money drowns him out. It isn't just that money talks. It talks louder and longer and drowns out the citizen's hoarse whisper.[6]

Later in his book, Gardner also warned about the growing power of banks:

> The growing concentration of economic power deserves special attention, and not only because, unlike most other institutional investors, banks have a lively interest in control of the companies in which they invest. The power of banks is greatly extended by their capacity to vote the portfolios of their trust accounts.[7]

In a few years Common Cause was able to boast a membership numbering 350,000 and a yearly budget of $6,000,000 becoming the biggest spender among Washington lobbies. One of its first victories was passage of an election reform bill limiting personal contributions to political candidates to $1,000. This seemed strange as it gave the media a big advantage over common people when it came to influencing an election. Since big money controls the media, why give them an even greater advantage? The answer was that Common Cause was controlled by very uncommon people.

As it turned out, the chairman, John Gardner, was on the board of trustees of the Rockefeller Brother's Fund, and the board of directors of Shell Oil, the world's second largest oil company. He was also on the boards of New York Telephone Company, American Airlines, and Time Incorporated. Gardner neglected to mention any of this when he prepared his biography for *Who's Who In America*. He also forgot to mention that he was a member of the CFR, which, of course, is the premier organization of America's elite.

The dedicated commoners who put up the money to launch Common Cause were none other than the Rockefellers. This was reported by Gary Allen in the March 1975 issue of *American Opinion*:

> Buried deep in the records of the Senate clerk . . . is a lobbyist's report filed by Gardner showing receipts for the last quarter of 1970. The largest donor was John D. Rockefeller III, who anted up twenty-five thousand dollars; David Rockefeller gave ten thousand dollars; Martha Rockefeller provided another ten thousand; Chase Manhattan Bank gave five thousand dollars; kindly Amory Houghton Jr. of the Rockefeller Foundation provided ten thousand; Nelson Rockefeller gave a guarded five hundred dollars; J. Richardson Dilworth, the family's financial advisor, gave five hundred; A. Meyer, senior partner, Lazard Freres and Company, the Rothschild's U.S. bank, provided ten thousand dollars; A.E. Friedman, a partner in the Rocke-

feller-allied Kuhn, Loeb and Company, gave a thousand; and, the list of the Establishment's super-rich goes on and on and on.[8]

Many large American companies also contributed to Common Cause such as Ford Motor Company, Allied Chemical, and Time Incorporated. With this kind of backing, naturally Common Cause received excellent news coverage.

It should be evident to the American people that something is wrong when such financial elite use their money to back an organization that is supposedly working against their interests and for the interests of the "little people."

Chapter 10

Money Manipulation and Legalized Plunder

As a result of the Saving and Loan crisis, the decade of the 1980s saw one of the largest transfers of wealth in the history of mankind. This transfer of wealth can rightly be described as legalized plunder. The *American Heritage Dictionary* defines "plunder" as, "To seize wrongfully or by force;..." In this case the law was used to wrongfully seize other men's property.

The story began when the U.S. government unconstitutionally became involved in the market place. Much of this came about as a result of creation of the great depression of 1929 and the following drive to socialize America upon the part of powerful money manipulators. Congress then created; (1) the Federal Home Loan Banks to make low-interest loans to member savings and loans; (2) the Federal Saving and Loan Insurance Corporation (FSLIC) to provide insurance for depositors; (3) the Federal Home Loan Bank Board (FHLBB) to oversee the system. This led to the establishment of the giant savings and loan industry that was to see financial disaster over 40 years later.

Trouble began in the late 1970s and the early 1980s when S&Ls began losing their depositors to financial

Money Manipulation and Legalized Plunder

institutions that paid higher rates of interest. At a time when government regulations limited S&Ls to paying 5.5 percent, the interest rate on money market funds rose to over 15 percent. As a result, S&L depositors left in droves. This left S&Ls with assets of long-term fixed-rate mortgages and liabilities of short-term deposits withdrawable on demand. S&Ls typically held only about $5 of assets for every $100 of deposit liabilities; therefore, by the early 1980s, most of the S&L industry was insolvent.

The government then stepped in to try to solve the problems resulting from its involvement in the marketplace. Congress passed two major pieces of legislation —the Depository Institutions Deregulation and Monetary Control Act of 1980 and the Garn-St. Germain Depository Institutions Act of 1982. The main features of this legislation were; (1) Elimination of deposit and interest-rate restrictions; (2) Reduction of exposure to interest-rate risk; (3) Increased investment powers; (4) Increased deposit insurance; (5) Reduced capital requirements; (6) Organizational form changes. This gave S&Ls the chance to earn more income for their depositors. It also attracted opportunists to the industry who had little experience, and gave the Federal Reserve increased power over depository institutions.

Conditions for the industry actually improved for a while as S&Ls invested heavily in real estate. This was encouraged by Congress with special tax breaks beginning in 1981. Newly encouraged investments in high-yield bonds (called junk bonds) also led to improved financial conditions for a small percentage of the industry.

This all changed when the real estate market began to decline. Then, Congress pulled the rug out from under S&Ls by eliminating many of the 1981 tax breaks with tax reforms in 1986. A wave of defaults in real estate loans resulted. However, many S&L operators had already diversified into other investments.

Congressional response to the failure of some S&Ls was to create the Financial Institutions Reform, Recovery and Enforcement Act (FIRREA) of 1989. This law established two new agencies within the executive branch: the Office of Thrift Supervision (OTS) to regulate and determine the solvency of thrifts, and the Resolution Trust Corporation (RTC) to manage seized thrifts and sell off their assets. The problem had been created and now the solution was put forth, —more government.

Author Mollie Dickenson had this to say about the Resolution Trust Corporation:

> All told, the RTC has spent $130 billion of taxpayers' money and sold $400 billion worth of seized assets. Many of these assets, sold at discounts of 30 to 40 percent (taxpayers make up the difference so thrift depositors can be reimbursed in full), have ended up in the hands of wealthy individuals (Texas investor Robert Bass, Revlon chief executive Ron Perelman), corporations (GE Capital Corp., Ford Motor Credit

Co.), and partnerships managed by Wall Street firms (Merrill Lynch, Goldman Sachs). Together, these asset sales constitute one of the largest transfers of wealth in U.S. history.[1]

Worth magazine quoted Robert O'Brien, former chief executive of a New Jersey thrift as saying, "Having to spend $150 billion allowed the administration to create an enormous political fiefdom."[2] FIRREA also turned the tables on the thrift business, redefining previously allowed investments, such as real estate, as impermissible. *Worth* magazine went on to state:

> S&Ls effectively had up to five years to sell all real estate included in their capital; during that time they had to discount the value of these properties by ever-increasing percentages. Junk bonds were also written down and had to be sold. Also, uninsured capital notes, commonly sold to bolster S&Ls' financial positions, were now disallowed.
> FIRREA also reneged on the contracts that many S&Ls had struck with the government when they agreed to take over failed thrifts, contracts that had allowed thrifts to count as assets the money owed to depositors of the failed institution, their negative net worth. This accounting mechanism, known as regulatory goodwill, had saved millions in taxpayer money throughout the '80s. "It was an enormous benefit to the government," says *Bank Bailout Litigation News's* Simon. But FIRREA took it away. As a result, many thrifts instantly found themselves out of capital compliance.
> As if FIRREA weren't enough, many thrifts weren't even given a chance to sell their real estate or junk

bonds. The OTS marched in and arbitrarily wrote down the assets, making the S&Ls "undercapitalized" and subject to seizure. Often, OTS employees refused to let S&Ls sell assets.[3]

Edward Morris, former CEO of Germania Savings and Loan in St. Louis, had this to say: "Regulators arbitrarily define your capital away, take over your bank, sell your assets for pennies on the dollar, then, coming up way short of money to pay off depositors and investors, say, 'See, we said this was a worthless thrift!'"[4] As a reward for carrying out this assault against hundreds of thrifts, OTS and RTC regulators were paid annual salaries up to $158,000. Among federal workers, only the president, vice president, and chief justice are paid more.

One of the most tragic cases to come out of the S&L scandal was the story of Scott Cone who became head man at Landmark Land company when regulators stepped in and fired his boss. After working for two years to keep Landmark out of the hands of hostile thrift regulators, Cone found himself out of a job and banned for life from banking. Faced with mounting legal bills and government suits, on a Sunday night before Thanksgiving, Scott Cone put the family shotgun to his head and pulled the trigger. Later Cone was exonerated from any wrongdoing, but that was little comfort to his widow and two daughters.

There were some cases of criminal violations of the law and high living with S&L funds. However, this was not the cause of the S&L crisis. In one of the most outstanding examples of extravagant living, the case of Donald Dixon of Vernon Savings and Loan, only .05 percent of Vernon's collapse had been attributed to Dixon's unlawful conduct.

Unforseen regional market changes created problems for some S&Ls. This was true in the case of Lincoln Saving and Loan in California. Although it was a California company, most of Lincoln's assets were in Arizona real estate. When the Arizona real estate market fell in the late 1980s, Lincoln's assets greatly declined. What is seldom mentioned is that every major Arizona thrift in existence in 1985 subsequently failed or was acquired. None survived as an independent entity. This was overlooked in the haste to find a scapegoat for Lincoln's problems. Most S&Ls could have survived had they not been pushed over the cliff and seized.

In addition to the S&L scandal, the 1980s also saw a period of government involvement in scandal in another area of finance. This was described by University of Chicago Law School Professor Daniel Fischel in his 332 page book *Payback: The Conspiracy to Destroy Michael Milken and His Financial Revolution*. This story, compiled from Fischel's first hand experience, reveals frightening examples of unrestrained government power used to destroy competitive free enterprise and plunder the wealth of the accused.

It began with what professor Fischel referred to as "The Restructuring of Corporate America" and centered around the phenomenal success of the firm of Drexel Burnham Lambert under the direction of Michael Milken. This period gave rise to the high-yield bond market that made possible the growing number of corporate takeovers during the 1980s. The losers were often old line Wall Street insiders. The winners were self-made outsiders like Michael Milken.

What was labeled as "junk bonds" were anything but "junk" as these high-yield bonds made fortunes for many companies. Until the government succeeded in destroying the market, on the average, no one lost money on these bonds. Government regulators even recommended their purchase by troubled S&Ls. Later, high-yield bonds were blamed for the S&L crisis although only about 450 of the approximately 4,000 S&Ls in existence in 1980 ever held any high-yield bonds. Between March of 1985 to December of 1991 the percentage of S&L assets held in high-yield bonds averaged less than one percent (actually .75%). This made it impossible for high-yield bonds to be the major factor in S&L failures. In spite of this, high-yield bonds were used as a scapegoat.

The United States General Accounting Office released a report in early March 1989 that concluded that high-yield bonds were not responsible for the S&L crisis. It stated:

> Compared to other fixed income investments, such as Treasury and investment grade bonds, high yield bonds

have a higher risk of default. However, studies by academics and investment bankers show that from 1977 to 1987 high yield bonds have provided investors higher net returns than these other investments because their relatively high yields have outweighed the additional losses from default....

A review of FHLBB data and discussions with its officials showed only one case in 1985 where high yield bond investments appeared to have been a factor in a thrift failure. However, in that case, mismanagement of the institution's high yield bond portfolio was only one part of a broader pattern of unsafe lending and investment practices leading to the institution's collapse.[5]

Blaming the S&L crisis on high-yield bonds served two purposes. It shifted attention away from government's bungling that created the problem in the first place, and aided the nationwide campaign to destroy Drexel and Michael Milken. This relentless campaign was waged throughout the 80s, labeling the 80s as a "decade of greed" with Drexel and Milken as central targets. Even the *Wall Street Journal* joined in the chorus of wolves howling for the blood of Drexel and Milken.

Referring to Milken's wealth, David Rockefeller commented that, "such an extraordinary income inevitably raises questions as to whether there isn't something unbalanced in the way our financial system is working."[6] This is an interesting comment coming from one of the world's richest men. Perhaps Mr. Rockefeller believes that only a privileged few should be allowed to obtain great wealth.

There were several factors that probably caused the mighty power of government to be unleashed against Drexel and Milken. For one thing, the results of the financial revolution of the 80s were all beneficial. The Dow Jones Industrial Average tripled during the 1980s, and investors made close to $1 trillion from restructuring transactions. The ratio of the market value of debt to the market value of assets remained remarkably constant during the 1980s. During this period the total value of corporate equities also increased dramatically.

One of the results of financial control being shifted away from the New York banks and into the hands of smaller investors was a net increase of millions of American jobs during the 1980s. A major benefit of the high-yield bond market gave corporations the ability to borrow directly from investors rather than borrowing from banks. This also gave investors more control over poorly performing and entrenched corporate managers.

Corporations being able to borrow from investors was especially beneficial in that such borrowing did not contribute to inflation because the money already existed. In contrast, approximately 90 percent of the money borrowed from the banks is created through the inflationary process.

Everything about the financial revolution of the 1980s was contrary to what CFR and Trilateral insiders like David Rockefeller had planned for the United States.

Money Manipulation and Legalized Plunder

What occurred did not fit into the plan for a New World Order. Perhaps even Michael Milken didn't realize what he was up against.

One of the methods used to destroy those outside the Establishment's financial kingdom is known as *ex post facto* law, which simply means passing a law and making it retroactive. Prosecution for *ex post facto* crimes is forbidden by the Constitution, but that fact was ignored in many of the government's prosecutions during the 1980s.

Another weapon used by government prosecutors was the newly created crime called "Insider Trading." Congress made this possible by passage of two laws, the Insider Trading Sanctions Act of 1984 (ITSA), and the Insider Trading and Securities Fraud Enforcement Act of 1988 (ITSFEA). The irony of this legislation was that Congress never defined the practice of insider trading. The Securities and Exchange Commission (SEC) opposed efforts to define the term, emphasizing the dangers of "freezing into law either a definition which is too broad, or too narrow to deal with emerging issues." Congress agreed and passed ITSFEA by a vote of 410-0 in the House and a voice vote in the Senate.

Professor Fischel commented that, "The ITSFEA thus gave regulators and prosecutors maximum power and discretion to prosecute whomever they choose for essentially whatever reasons they choose."[7] Many men were fined and imprisoned for violation of a law without a definition of what they had violated. Professor Fischel argued that:

> Criminalizing an activity without defining it runs counter to powerful traditions in American law. Defendants have a constitutional right to fair notice that behavior is criminal. Unlike certain highly repressive Communist or other dictatorial nations, America has no tradition of common-law crimes, where courts can declare conduct criminal on a case-by-case basis. The Supreme Court declared such common-law crimes unconstitutional more than 150 years ago. Even Congress has no power to decree that individuals can be criminally prosecuted for conduct that was not criminal at the time it occurred.[8]

Another routine trading practice also redefined as criminal was known as "Stock Parking." The problem with this was explained by Fischel: "The term is nowhere defined in the securities laws. Nor is there any other law that defines, let alone criminalizes, the 'parking' of stock. Under common usage, stock parking occurs when a nominee purchases securities from or on behalf of the true owner on the understanding that the securities will later be bought back by the owner, who bears the risk of gain or loss."[9] This did not prevent the theory of stock parking from becoming a favorite for criminal prosecution during the 1980s. Ivan Boesky was sentenced to three years in prison, and fined $100 million for this alleged "crime."

Money Manipulation and Legalized Plunder

The ultimate weapon used to destroy financial institutions was the Racketeer Influenced and Corrupt Organizations Act (RICO). This legislation, passed by Congress in 1970, gave the government sweeping new powers. One of these was the power to freeze a defendant's assets at the time of indictment and confiscate them after conviction. It allows the government to seize entire businesses connected, even indirectly, with a defendant at the time of indictment, before any proof of guilt. In effect, RICO made the government prosecutor, judge, and jury.

On August 4, 1988, the government indicted Jay Regan and four other officers of Princeton/Newport for violation of RICO. This was the first time RICO had ever been used against a financial institution. As a result, Princeton/Newport was destroyed.

After the example of RICO being used to destroy Princeton/Newport, it was used to pressure Drexel leaders to plead guilty to six felonies and pay a record penalty of $650 million in fines and restitution. On Tuesday, February 13, 1990, Drexel declared bankruptcy.

Milken was also pressured to plead guilty to six felonies and pay a $200 million fine and $400 million to compensate "victims." In November 1990 he was sentenced to serve ten years in prison. This was later reduced to twenty-four months. Professor Fischel had this to say about the episode: "After the most thorough investigation of any individual's business practices in history, the government came up with nothing. In fact, the government never established that Milken's 'crimes' were anything other than routine business practices common in the industry."[10]

What has happened in the high-yield bond market since 1990 served to prove the folly of the drive to destroy the market. It bounced back to produce phenomenal returns, far outperforming returns generated by other bond investments or the stock market. The government succeeded in driving Drexel and Milken out of business, but it did not destroy the high-yield bond market. Many of those who were in favor of putting Drexel and Milken out of business stepped in to fill the place Drexel and Milken had filled in the market.

Professor Fischel concluded that:

> The so-called Wall Street and savings and loan scandals of the 1980s wouldn't have occurred if the government hadn't intervened. This important point should not be forgotten as America approaches the twenty-first century.[11]

CHAPTER 11

BANKING AND THE NEW WORLD ORDER

Much has been written about and commented on in reference to the mark of the beast referred to in New Testament Scripture. First mentioned in Rev. 13:16 to18, conditions are depicted whereby all who did not receive this mark on their forehead or hand would not be allowed to buy or sell. It is generally supposed that the word "all" refers to all human inhabitants of earth. It is more likely that it refers to a range of social and economic strata in highly developed nations rather than the sum total of all people. Another indication that "all" refers to a range rather than a total, is that some did not receive such a mark and thus escaped the dire consequences pronounced on those who did.

While some did become martyrs rather than submit to the mark of the beast Rev. 20:4, others were victorious over the Beast and his mark. This is expressed plainly in Revelation 15:2, "And I saw as it were a sea of glass mingled with fire: and them that had gotten the victory over the beast, and over his image, and over his mark, and over the number of his name, stand on the sea of glass, having the harps of God." All seven of the major

English translations of Scripture say essentially the same thing. *The American Standard, Living Bible,* and *New International* versions refer to those who were "victorious" over the beast. The *Revised Standard* refers to "those who had conquered the beast." The *Simple English* version refers to those who had "defeated the wild animal."

The Greek word for "all" used in Rev. 13:16, "he causeth all" is πᾶς (pas). It is a broad term and can mean several things such as: all matter of, as many as, whosoever, as well as the whole.

Such control over part of the human beings on earth could be possible with a central bank controlling the money system. With a computerized system of centrally controlled fiat money, simply removing a person's account numbers would have that effect. The foundation for just such a worldwide banking structure was laid in Bretton Woods, New Hampshire in 1944. In his book *Financial Terrorism: Hijacking America Under the Threat of Bankruptcy* John F. McManus explained its creation:

> What's the Bretton Woods system? In July 1944, many of the world's prominent bankers and government planners met at Bretton Woods, New Hampshire at the invitation of President Franklin Roosevelt. Their deliberations produced the UN's International Monetary Fund and the post-world War II monetary system which has been working for almost half a century to create a centrally controlled economic system for the planet. The

IMF has also regularly created sufficient turmoil to topple governments and steer nations into the type of government-directed economic planning it favors.

A good understanding of the thrust of the IMF can be gained through awareness of the individuals who guided it into existence. The April 20, 1971 issue of *The American Banker* reported: "The main architects of the Fund were Harry Dexter White and John Maynard Keynes (later Lord Keynes) of the American and British Treasuries.... Keynes had written about a world central bank as early as 1930, while White had been instructed by the U.S Treasury only a week after Pearl Harbor to start drafting plans for an international stabilization fund after the war."[1]

The late Gary Allen gave more details about the background of the main architects of the International Monetary Fund (IMF) in his book *Say "No" To the New World Order:*

> John Maynard Keynes was the darling of the British Fabian Society, the gang of socialist conspirators who had taken over and wrecked Great Britain. An aggressive homosexual, Keynes also promulgated a queer brand of economics which, among other things, strongly encouraged unrestrained government spending and deliberate budget deficits as a cure for inflation-caused recessions....
>
> Harry Dexter White was a bird of an even more crimson hue. While all the standard histories of the IMF fail to mention it, [he] was at once a member of the Council on Foreign Relations and a dedicated Soviet agent. White had moved into various positions of impor-

tance in the U.S. Treasury Department where he carefully laid out plans for a new monetary order....
On November 6, 1953, Attorney General Herbert Brownell revealed that Harry Dexter White's "spying activities for the Soviet Government were reported in detail by the FBI to the White House... in December of 1945. In the face of this information, and incredible though it may seem, President Truman went ahead and nominated White, who was then Assistant Secretary of the Treasury, for the even more important position of executive director for the United States in the International Monetary Fund..."[2]

The Council on Foreign Relations (CFR) was a major force behind the creation of the International Monetary Fund (IMF) and the World Bank. Incorporated in New York on July 29, 1921, the objective of the CFR was the merger of the United States into a World Government. Its chief architect was Edward Mandel House who called for "Socialism as dreamed of by Karl Marx." The organization that House founded was to become the hidden government of the United States. From its original membership list of 210 men, the CFR has grown to include 3,000 of the most prominent leaders in America. For decades it has controlled United States foreign policy and has operated on the secret side of history, shielded from public view.

Another important and powerful organization behind the IMF and World Bank is the Trilateral Commission. It was founded by David Rockefeller in 1973 and is made up of some of the leading financial figures of the

Banking and the New World Order

world. It is also dedicated to World Government. As stated by Michel Camdessus, director of the IMF, "This is about power and money."[3] The IMF and World Bank are indeed about power and money. They are also about robbery, and the transfer of the wealth of the world into the hands of a few powerful international bankers. Mexico is an example of how this is accomplished, the prime ingredient being debt.

Mexico is controlled by one of the longest ruling political parties in the world. It was also the first nation in this hemisphere to fall to a Communist dictatorship.[4] As is generally the case in a socialist country, the government has stayed alive financially by borrowing money, most of it coming from banks in the United States. The banks were eager to accommodate because it involved no risk on their part, as the money was pure fiat created out of nothing, with repayment guaranteed by the U.S. government.

A major crisis developed on December 20, 1994 when President Zedillo announced a 13% devaluation of the peso. The peso was then allowed to float freely against the dollar, resulting in a 39% plunge. Not only was the general economy in a shambles, the government couldn't pay the interest on its previous loans from Wall Street. This was the fifth time Mexico was to find herself in such a position, and the fifth time it was to be bailed out. The first time was in 1982, then 1985, 1988, and 1989. By this time Mexico, with a national economy about the size of Los Angeles, was in debt $100 billion.

The New York firm of Goldman Sachs was one of those most involved in Mexican finance. As it turned out, the U.S. Secretary of the Treasury, Robert Rubin, happened to have a $100 million dollar interest in Goldman. As a former co-chairman of the firm he earned $26 million in 1993. Mr. Rubin went to work to help arrange a $40 billion bailout so Mexico could pay the interest on its loans from the New York banks. This bailout was backed by CFR member Newt Gingrich, CFR member Bill Clinton, and Senator Bob Dole. Rubin's name had also been added to the CFR membership list. Perhaps it was just a coincidence that Goldman Sacks personnel were some of the largest supporters of the Clinton presidential campaign.

The result of all of this has been a financial takeover of Mexico by international bankers, which was the goal in the first place. Before NAFTA, only 18 foreign banks were allowed to operate in Mexico. Now, everything is wide open with the way clear for Wall Street banks to take over as a step toward world government. Where the IMF and World Bank fits into all of this was explained in *The New American* by Jane H. Ingraham:

> In reality, the hidden agenda of the IMF's creators called for the building of world socialism. This was to be accomplished through the elimination of gold and its restricting discipline from world finance and the eventual creation of a world currency based on nothing. A world bank would then be able to inflate at will (producing a uniform worldwide rate of inflation) and control the

world's nations (stripped of their own currencies) through the control of money and credit.[5]

Ingraham also explained the results of the creation of the IMF and World Bank:

> In spite of the hundreds of billions of dollars in Western aid handed out all over the earth since the end of World War II, not a single instance can be cited of any country that has been raised up by it. This, after all, has been the intent. The real objectives are obvious: to redistribute the wealth of the West and lower our own standard of living preparatory to world merger, and to control emerging national leaders (usually despotic) who become pawns in the game once they are hooked on high-living and wealth embezzled from aid funds.[6]

The international bankers long ago began looking ahead to the time when they would need an all powerful United Nation's military force to compel all nations to accept their financial edicts. This began with a program to disarm all nations and create a UN army. Although their program is now far advanced, it can still be stopped.

To finally spring the trap, the money manipulators may revert to the age-old revolutionary ploy of creating a crisis and then offering the solution. The crisis would be financial. The solution would be a World Bank to issue a world currency. To silence opposition and lure the gullible, the manipulators might even shock the world by offering a partially gold-backed currency. This would

The Secret Side of Money

only last long enough for the transition to be completed. When any nation rebelled, the UN army would be used to bring "peace"; and the world pictured in George Orwell's *Nineteen Eighty-Four* would have arrived.

In order to accomplish their plans for world control, the powerful elitists have used patient gradualism as one of their weapons. They have also gone to great efforts to neutralize the opposition of good people who would normally oppose them. In order to throw light on this, we need to go back to the roots of the present-day scheme for control of the world's monetary system.

In 1966 a 1,384-page book written by Georgetown University professor Carroll Quigley became available. In this book, *Tragedy and Hope,* Quigley described the creation of a "secret society" by Cecil Rhodes and his friends in 19th Century England. Quigley was not opposed to this group and stated that he had studied it for twenty years and was even allowed to examine its secret papers. According to Quigley this was their plan:

> [T]he powers of financial capitalism had another far reaching aim, nothing less than to create a world system of financial control in private hands able to dominate the political system of each country and the economy of the world as a whole. This system was to be controlled in a feudalist fashion by the central banks of the world acting in concert, by secret agreements arrived at in frequent private meetings and conferences . . . .[7]

Banking and the New World Order

During the 19th century, Cecil Rhodes became one of the richest men in the world by obtaining a monopoly over the diamond output of South Africa and most of its gold as well. This was accomplished with financial backing from the Bank of England and the Rothschilds. Most of his money was spent working for world control by a financial elite. Quigley explained how this money was used:

> The Rhodes Scholarships, established by the terms of Cecil Rhodes' seventh will, are known to everyone. What is not so widely known is that Rhodes in five previous wills left his fortune to form a secret society, which was to devote itself to the preservation and expansion of the British Empire. And what does not seem to be known to anyone is that this secret society was created by Rhodes and his principal trustee, Lord Milner, and continues to exist to this day.... In his book on Rhodes' wills, he [Stead, who was a member of the inner circle] wrote in one place: "Mr. Rhodes was more than the founder of a dynasty. He aspired to be the creator of one of those vast semi-religious, quasi-political associations which, like the Society of Jesus, have played so large a part in the history of the world.[8]

After the death of Cecil Rhodes his secret society was controlled by Lord Alfred Milner, Governor-General and High Commissioner of South Africa. As a director of a number of public banks and a corporate precursor as the leader of England's Midland Bank, he was one of the most powerful political and financial figures of his time.

Milner recruited young men from Oxford University and Toynbee Hall into Rhodes' secret society. Quigley tells of Milner's success:

> Through his influence these men were able to win influential posts in government and international finance and became the dominant influence in British imperial and foreign affairs up to 1939.... In 1909-1913 they organized semi-secret groups, known as Round Table Groups, in the chief British dependencies and the United States.... Money for the widely ramified activities of this organization came ... chiefly from the Rhodes Trust itself, and from wealthy associates . . . [9]

The Rhodes group, known as the Round Table, was behind the establishment of the Council on Foreign Relations in the United States. A Rhodes scholarship program was set up at Oxford to train promising young men from the United States and England.

It was only natural that Oxford University would be chosen as a training center for Rhodes scholars because it was at Oxford University that Cecil Rhodes was sold the idea of a ruling elite. The man responsible for his indoctrination was a rich socialist professor by the name of John Ruskin. Rhodes then spent most of his life promoting the philosophy of Ruskin. Oxford University also became a center for anti-Christian socialist indoctrination.

Chapter 12

Regaining a Sound Perspective

What is the hindrance that keeps the American people from freeing themselves from economic slavery? It is basically the same problem that existed in the days of Israel when the prophet Hosea lamented, "My people are destroyed for lack of knowledge:..." Hosea 4:6. Isaiah said, "Therefore my people are gone into captivity, because they have no knowledge:..." Isaiah 5:13. Unfortunately, the vast majority of the American people have little or no knowledge of money or its manipulation by bankers and politicians. The lack of knowledge and loss of a true perspective of world conditions is not an accident, but the result of design by an elite who wish to control the destiny of all mankind.

This design has included clever and long-range propaganda, especially in the religious field. This area has always been a prime target because it is usually religious people who are the ones who oppose collectivism. Control of religion is also sought in order to spread false ideals because men can often be convinced of anything if it is clothed in religious language. This is a weakness recognized and often used by communists, socialists, and con-artists. Jesus expressed it this way, "...For the children of this world are in their generation wiser than the children of light" Luke 16:8.

One of the methods used to neutralize opposition to collectivist's plans is to promote the idea that world events are controlled by prophecy and therefore impossible to change. The next step is to convince believers that there is no need for concern because they will suddenly be removed from the earth, just before disaster occurs. Its proponents teach that; (1) the evils of our day are inevitable events; (2) Christians are promised escape; (3) this could happen (the rapture) at any moment. This is the doctrine of dispensationalism. It is noteworthy to consider that the founders of this new doctrine were not very good prophets as all of them died a natural death and were buried. Not one saw the imminent rapture he taught. This relatively recent theory of the pre-tribulation "rapture" of the church began in 1830. For eighteen centuries of church history it was unheard of.

Their theory is also refuted by the results of the Satanic war waged throughout the 20th century against all those who believe in God as Creator. This has not only resulted in the death of millions of Christians, and the near destruction of the Church in a score of nations, it has also resulted in the death of millions of Jews and Muslims. For a better understanding of this Satanic war against those who believe in God as Creator, we recommend our own book *The Secret Side of History: Mystery Babylon and the New World Order.* It is available from

Regaining a Sound Perspective

LTAA Communications, P.O. Box 403092, Hesperia, California 92345. The price is $12.00 postpaid.

The teaching of dispensationalism can be traced back to a Pentecostal group led by Margaret Macdonald in Port Glasgow, Scotland in 1830. Macdonald's theory was picked up by John Nelson Darby who formed a group known as the Brethren, or Plymouth Brethren, after the town of their origin in England.

Darby had been an Anglican priest but left the Anglican Church to spread the dispensationalism doctrine. He came to the United States and between 1862 and 1877 spread this new doctrine in several large cities, principally in the midwest. A series of annual summer conferences that began in 1875 enabled Darby to influence many important American church leaders. These events were known as the Niagara Bible Conferences because they were held at Niagara-on-the-Lake, Ontario. It was here that Darby met two men who became leaders in his movement. One was Arno C. Gaebelein; the other was Cyrus Ingerson Scofield.

Because of the publication of the *Scofield Reference Bible*, the name of Cyrus Scofield became a household word to millions of Protestants. More than 50,000 words of Scofield's teaching were printed on over 500 pages of the *Scofield Reference Bible*. Because these notes were on the same pages as Scripture, they were often considered as valid as Scripture.

That Oxford University became a center for anti-Christian socialist indoctrination is not surprising. What is surprising is that Oxford University press published the *Scofield Reference Bible*. Also surprising is that Scofield went to Oxford to do research for his work.

This was such a puzzle to author Joseph M. Canfield, a former dispensationalist, that he decided to investigate the background of Cyrus I. Scofield. The results of his research, are recorded in his book *The Incredible Scofield And His Book*. One of the first things he discovered was that, unlike most well known religious leaders, very little had been published about Cyrus I. Scofield. Oxford University Press in New York published a book by Charles G. Trumbull entitled *The Life of C.I. Scofield*, but it contained many questionable accounts and omitted many significant events.

Cyrus Scofield was born in Lenawee County, Michigan on August 19, 1843, the son of Elias and Abigail Scofield. When 17, he was visiting his sister in Tennessee at the time the Civil War started. Cyrus joined the Confederate military by enlisting in the 7th Regiment of Tennessee Infantry. After his release from the Infantry he went to St. Louis where another sister resided and began to work into a law career. Here he married Leontine Cerre on September 21, 1866. Later he and his family moved to Kansas, where he became involved in the practice of law and politics. In 1871 he was elected to the Lower House of the Kansas Legislature. Upon the recommendation of his former law partner John J. Ingalls, then a member of the 43rd Congress, President Grant appointed Scofield to the office of United States

District Attorney for the District of Kansas. Scofield was only 29 at the time of his appointment. When he took the oath of office, as an ex-Confederate soldier, he swore that he had:

> ... never voluntarily borne arms against the United States since I have been a citizen thereof, that I have voluntarily given no aid, countenance, counsel or encouragement to persons engaged in armed hostility thereto ... that I have not yielded a voluntary support to any pretended government authority, power of constitution, within the United States, hostile or inimical thereto....[1]

This was actually perjury. Scofield's career as district attorney was short-lived and he resigned after about six months of service amid charges of corruption. When Scofield presided over the funeral of Dwight L. Moody, this amazing article appeared in the December 28, 1899 *Kansas City Journal:*

> The pastor who delivered the sermon and presided at the funeral of Dwight L. Moody, the famous evangelist, was Rev. C. I. Scofield. Some of the readers of The Journal may have recognized this name, but probably few will recall that Scofield was formerly of Kansas and figured prominently in politics....
> Scofield landed in Nemaha County in 1872, just in time to be nominated on the Republican ticket for member of the legislature. He was elected, and, though ostensibly a supporter of Senator Pomeroy, he became largely instrumental in causing the election of Ingalls.

Indeed, he was recognized as one of the foremost leaders in the Ingalls camp and by some as Ingall's personal representative, and in reward for his services he was made United States district attorney for the state. But he did not hold this office long. He was ousted in disgrace on account of some shady financial transactions which left him indebted in a number of thousands to a score of prominent Republicans. One of his victims once said to Topics: "The way Scofield got our money — and he plucked $2,000 of mine — was by intimating that it was needed by Senator Ingalls, who would see that it was paid. We knew that Ingalls was good, and we supposed that on account of his official position he did not care to be known in a money-borrowing transaction and was doing the business through a friend."

In due time, however, the shady nature of Scofield's financial transactions became known to Ingalls and the money lenders and then followed an explosion which compelled Scofield to resign his federal office and leave the state. From Kansas he went to St. Louis, and, shortly after his arrival there, he was lodged in jail on a charge of forgery, preferred by his own sister. At this point in his checkered life began his religious career, for when he emerged from confinement he was an enthusiastic Salvationist.[2]

The religious career of Scofield blossomed over night. Suddenly, with little or no theological background, he became pastor and teacher. Apparently, he awarded himself the title of Doctor of Divinity since there is no record of any institution having awarded him this degree.

After his resignation as Attorney General, Scofield separated from his wife and ended up in St. Louis.

Trumbull said that he went to St. Louis to practice law, but there is no record that he was ever a member of the St. Louis Bar. His abandonment of his wife and two daughters made it necessary for his wife to go to work to support herself and the children. When Leontine filed for divorce on December 9, 1881, she charged that Cyrus:

> . . has been guilty of gross neglect of duty and has failed to support this plaintiff or her said children, or to contribute thereto, and has made no provision for them for food, clothing or a home, or in any manner performed his duty in the support of said family although he was able to do so.[3]

The matter was finally settled on December 8, 1883. The decree stated that Cyrus "was not a fit person to have custody of the children" and forbade him to interfere with their rearing. At the very time he was involved in the divorce case he was ordained to the Christian ministry. Had this been known, he probably would not have been ordained. Also unadvertised was Scofield's membership in the high-society Lotus Club in New York, a most unlikely place for a minister.

It also appears that Scofield was anything but a successful lawyer in St. Louis, as related by Trumbull. He did spend time in court (1877-1879), but as a defendant in at least two forgery cases. This was revealed in court records. Trumbull placed Scofield's conversion as taking place in his law office in 1879. However, there is no record of Cyrus ever having a law office in St. Louis.

However the case, Cyrus Scofield did have a sufficiently tainted reputation to become a subject of the press. With due regard to the fact that newspapers are not always champions of truth, Scofield's career was such that he did furnish them grist for their mill. Following is an example from the Topeka *Daily Capital* on August 27, 1881:

> Cyrus I. Scofield, formerly of Kansas, late lawyer, politician and shyster generally, has come to the surface again, and promises once more to gather around himself that halo of notoriety that has made him so prominent in the past. The last personal knowledge that Kansans have had of this peer among scalawags, was when about four years ago, after a series of forgeries and confidence games he left the state and a destitute family and took refuge in Canada. For a time he kept undercover nothing being heard of him until within the past two years when he turned up in St. Louis, where he had a wealthy widowed sister living who has generally come to the front and squared up Cyrus' little follies and foibles by paying good round sums of money. Within the past year however Cyrus committed a series of St. Louis forgeries that could not be settled so easily, and the erratic young gentleman was compelled to linger in the St. Louis jail for a period of six months.[4]

The main question that arouses suspicion is not whether one's life can be changed by religious conversion, but why such efforts have been made to conceal the background of such a prominent religious leader? And why has information about Scofield's history been so distorted? Another question is what forces were able to cause such a rapid rise in his career from one with such a background and little training to a chair of Bible history in Moody's Northfield Bible school?

It is most likely that powerful forces wanted Scofield's message to be publicized. How else could a little-known minister with one small book to his credit walk into the office of the most well-known publishers in the world and sign a contract for the publication of his work. Anyone acquainted with the publishing world knows this doesn't happen without some very important connections.

Whether by design or not, this turned out to be to the advantage of the money powers working to control the world because the doctrine of dispensationalism neutralized millions of good people who would otherwise have opposed them.

Nor have efforts to convince good people to acquiesce to evil been abandoned. Most would-be prophets of the end time ignore the real creators of the world's problems, preferring to dwell in a mystical no-mans land where nothing can be proved or disproved.

As Oxford University became a center of socialist teaching, Dallas Theological Seminary in Dallas, Texas became a center for dispensationalist doctrine. One of Scofield's longstanding goals was the founding of Dallas Theological Seminary. Books written by faculty and students of Dallas Theological Seminary promoting the end time rapture theory have sold in the millions of copies.

One example is a book written by the associate professor of Bible exposition at Dallas Theological Seminary, Dr. Charles H. Dyer. The title of the book is *The Rise of Babylon: Sign of the End Time*. It starts with a caption on the front cover that reads, "Startling photos from Iraq reveal that Saddam Hussein is rebuilding the lost city of Babylon. The Bible says Babylon will be rebuilt in the last days. Could ours be the last generation?"[5] Contrary to Dyer's teaching most students of O.T. Scripture accept the prophets Isaiah's words that, "It [Ancient Babylon] shall never be inhabited, neither shall it be dwelt in from generation to generation...." Isaiah 13:20.

To back up his statements about Babylon, Dyer quoted an article in the *New York Times* of October 11, 1990:

> Under President Saddam Hussein, one of the ancient world's most legendary cities has begun to rise again. More than an archaeological venture, the new Babylon is self-consciously dedicated to the idea that Nebuchadnezzar has a successor in Mr. Hussein, whose military prowess and vision will restore to Iraqis the glory their ancestors knew when all of what is now Iraq, Syria, Lebanon, Jordan, Kuwait, and Israel was under Babylonian control.[6]

The truth is that most of this was pure sensationalism. Except for a few buildings and a section of wall constructed for show, Ancient Babylon remains what it has been for centuries, a heap of ruins. Furthermore, much of the power that Saddam Hussein possesses was granted to him by the United States. This was revealed in *The New American* March 21, 1994 by William Jasper:

> Investigations by the House Banking Committee and journalists have carefully documented a sordid trail of treachery and treasonous actions by George Bush and his retinue before, during, and after the Persian Gulf War. One of the latest and most comprehensive expose's of this whole affair is provided in the new book, *Spider's Web: The Secret History of How the White House Illegally Armed Iraq*, by *Financial Times* of London correspondent Alan Friedman (reviewed in THE NEW AMERICAN, February 21, 1994). The U.S. provided, or assisted Iraq in obtaining cluster bombs, technology for nuclear enrichment, U.S.-designed munitions, missile technology, some $5 billion in loan guarantees, and much more. [7]

Iraq is in no way significant as a world power.

In the early 1970s a book was published claiming to explain major events as a fulfillment of Bible prophecy. In 1992 it was reprinted by Harper Paperbacks, a New York company, and now boasts 15 million copies in print. The book *The Late Great Planet Earth* was written by Hal Lindsey, a graduate of none other than the School of Theology of Dallas Theological Seminary. The co-author was Carole C. Carlson, a freelance writer. Among some publications quoted were such CFR dominated publications as, *The Los Angeles Times, Time,* and *Look*.

Among some of the personalities quoted are Dean Rusk (CFR), Bertrand Russell (Socialist), and Mao Tse-tung (Communist). The United Nations is also quoted as a source of "expert" information.

Many statements quoted to prove that the end of the world was near turned out to be farfetched at best, with little or no basis of fact. One quotation stated, "Unless mankind acts immediately, there will be a world wide famine in 1985, and the extinction of man within 75 years."[8] Another by Paul Ehrlich stated, "Mankind may be facing its final crisis. No action that we can take at this late date can prevent a great deal of future misery from starvation and environmental deterioration."[9] One of the most far-out statements came from Lindsey himself regarding Communist China, "Within a decade China alone will have the capacity to destroy one-third of the world's population just as John predicted."[10] This was supposed to be based upon a Bible prophecy. No place in Old or New Testament Scripture is the word "China" found. When 1980 arrived (a decade from the time the prediction was made) China was still a backward agrarian society, decades behind industrialized nations. It was not until the United States began to build up China's military and industry that any real progress was made toward modernization.

Another interesting prediction by Lindsey was that, "Israel will become fantastically wealthy and influential in the future."[11] To this date, 25 years later, Israel remains on international welfare as one of the largest recipients of United States foreign aid in the world. This is hardly the state of a nation "fantastically wealthy."

As to the United States, Lindsey stated, "Internal political chaos caused by student rebellions, and Communist subversion, will begin to erode the economy of our nation."[12] The truth is that bankers and politicians are the cause of the erosion of our economy, not students and communists. After blaming rising crime, poverty, illiteracy, illegitimacy, etc., on the "population explosion" Lindsey concludes that doomsday is here and man's only hope is the "Rapture" and, "We should be living like persons who don't expect to be around much longer,"[13] Needless to say, we are still around 25 years later.

In *Planet Earth 2000 A D.: Will Mankind Survive?* Lindsey parrots the New World Order line of ecological crisis, overpopulation, global warming, and deforestation. As to global warming he states, "There is essentially no longer much debate in scientific circles about whether a buildup of carbon dioxide is warming the Earth." He further stated, "What is the greenhouse effect? It is basically a threat to the Earth caused by the production of carbon dioxide. Man didn't begin heavy use of so-called 'fossil fuels' that have created this abundance of carbon dioxide until this century."[14]

In 100 years of measuring the mean (average) temperature of earth the maximum detectable change has been one-half of one degree Centigrade, and even this is debatable. There is no reliable scientific proof of global warming. As to man's use of CFCs causing global warming, the major amount in the atmosphere is caused by nature, and is out of the control of man.

As to ozone, Lindsey states, "Already more than 3 percent of the ozone layer has been destroyed."[15] He goes on to quote a United Nations "ozone expert." While there is variation in the ozone from season to season there is no reliable scientific data proving ozone depletion. For a reliable source of information showing that no catastrophic environmental threat exists, we recommend "The Resilient Earth" a special 66 page edition of *The New American 1993* fall issue. It is available from The New American, P.O. Box 8040, Appleton, WI 54913; $2.50 for one copy postpaid.

Citing such authorities as the Center for Disease Control, The World Health Organization (UN), and UNICEF (UN), the AIDS scare is also promoted. Lindsey stated, "Only in the late 1980s did we begin to realize that we were in the midst of plague as real and as dreadful as any the human race had ever experienced."[16] As we pointed out in chapter 9, evidence is fast accumulating that AIDS is a money-manufactured hoax.

The most blatant one world propaganda in *Planet Earth—2000 A.D.,* is the attack on Islam. Lindsey starts out by saying, "The greatest threat to freedom and world peace today—is Islamic fundamentalism."[17] He continues with, "...there is a quite new menace growing stronger every day—a force more explosive and dangerous than totalitarianism of the right or left. In fact, Islamic fundamentalism is actually billing itself as the successor to Marxism as the main agent of change in the world and the No. 1 challenge to the Judeo-Christian world order."[18]

In the March 21, 1994 issue of *The New American* Charles Carlson commented on the recent campaign against Islam and some of its origin:

> Examples of the vicious Islam-baiting media campaign are legion, but we have space here to present only a few of the more notorious and influential. Of these, the Spring 1993 *Foreign Affairs* offers a particularly noteworthy case. The keynote "debate" of that issue of the journal is framed by the article, "Is Islam a Threat?"' by CFR member Judith Miller, a *New York Times* writer and author of a new book entitled *The Arabs and Islam*. Ms. Miller's article makes negative generalizations about all of Islam, associating the vast majority of peaceful, law-abiding Muslims with the relatively small minority of those involved in outlaw activity. She depicts a warlike, united Islam, which she claims (without offering a shred of evidence) has executed a secret manifesto committing Islam to war against the West.[19]

In the same March 21, 1994 issue of *The New American* William Jasper commented on Council on Foreign Relations duplicity in attacking Islam:

> It would, no doubt, strike the uninformed as very odd then to learn that the same Council on Foreign Relations (CFR) operatives in government and the media

who are most loudly declaiming against the scourge of "militant" and "fundamentalist" Islam are indeed the very strategists who are most responsible for the policies and actions (both past and present) that have built, and continue to aid, the most fanatical, anti-American, "Islamic fundamentalist" regimes and organizations in the world today. Odd, that is, unless these regimes and organizations are serving a hidden purpose.[20]

Thus while the CFR attacks Islam in general, its operatives in government give aid to a small minority of extremists that claim to be true Muslims. This is the case in Iran, Iraq, Libya, Algeria, and now Afghanistan. The object is to justify United Nations military action in a host of Muslim countries. By March 1994, the UN war against Muslims had already resulted in 400,000 deaths in Iraq, Bosnia, and Somalia. These are called "peace" operations by the CFR-controlled news media. UN military forces are now in various stages of occupying at least ten Muslim Countries with plans to occupy 19 more areas, many of which are Muslim. It is understandable that the United States is blamed for the actions of the UN since U.S. taxpayers furnish 25 percent of the UN operating budget, and 30 percent of the UN war budget.

The truth is that the vast majority of Muslims are peaceful, God-fearing people who stand in the way of a New World Order as envisioned by the CFR. Furthermore, the greatest danger to world peace is the war-making capability in the hands of the United Nations.

Regaining a Sound Perspective

Another viewpoint of the prophets of doom that needs to be considered is the teaching that the presence of Israel in Palestine is a fulfillment of prophecy, and indicates that we live in the end time. The return of the Jews to Palestine was not a movement of Orthodox Jewish leaders but the result of the Zionist movement. One of the first promoters of the Zionist idea was Zvi Hirsch Kalischer during the period 1843 to 1862. The religious Jews of his time rejected his ideas. Another promoter was Moses Hess who published *Rome and Jerusalem* in 1862. Hess was a friend of Marx and Engles and a dedicated socialist. A few Jews, mostly from Russia, migrated to Palestine during the early part of the 1800s. It wasn't until 1882 when Baron Edmond de Rothschild began financing Jewish colonies in Palestine that Jewish migration really got under way. Most of the Orthodox Jews were suspicious of the Zionist movement and opposed it.

In 1904 a Russian-born Jewish chemist by the name of Chaim Weizmann (also a Zionist) went to England and settled in Manchester. Here he was introduced to powerful people in the government by C. P. Scott, editor of the left-wing newspaper the *Manchester Guardian*. Weizmann was instrumental in the issuing of the Balfour Declaration by the British government stating its desire to see a Jewish nation established in Palestine. Opposition from Orthodox Jews to the Balfour Declaration was so strong that it was not issued until Edward Mandel House, acting for President Wilson, sent a telegram to the British government declaring the support of the United States government for the declaration. The declaration was then issued and addressed to Lord Nathaniel Rothschild. Author Robert L. Pierce commented on the final events leading up to the establishment of the independent Nation of Israel:

> The final throes leading to the actual establishment of the independent Nation of Israel consisted of turmoil, violence, and terrorism involving the Jews, Arabs, and the British Army in Palestine. The chief features of this period were the assassination and terrorism inflicted by Jewish guerilla gangs against personnel of the British government and army. These tactics were disavowed, of course, by the leading Zionists, but the ultimate result of this pressure, combined with continued heavy illegal immigration of the "displaced persons" from eastern Europe into Palestine, was to "force" the Socialist British government to give up and withdraw its troops.[21]

In late 1947 the United Nations voted to partition Palestine into two parts, one was to be the new Nation of Israel. This was the final step.

Now, let's look at the personalities behind this entire movement. Arthur (Lord) Balfour, then the British foreign Minister, and a promoter of the Balfour Declaration was recommended as a member of the inner circle of Cecil Rhodes' secret society. This group planned to rule the world by control of the money system. The Rothschilds' involvement in designs for financial control over nations has been known for decades.

Regaining a Sound Perspective

Edward Mandel House, one of the founders of the CFR, was a dedicated socialist who spent his life working for world government. Also involved were the Warburgs, international bankers, Alfred Lord Milner, another member of Rhodes secret society, and John Maynard Keynes, a prominent socialist and one of the founders of the World Bank. These were some of the elite in socialist circles who promoted the world conditions that resulted in great suffering for the Jewish people, especially the rise of Hitler and Communism in Russia. All of them held ideas totally contrary to Orthodox Judaism. The players on the American side were essentially the same. This may account for some students of the Scripture believing that the present establishment of Israel in Palestine is not a fulfillment of Bible prophecy. However the case, the presence of the Jews in Palestine should not be used to persuade Americans to abandon efforts to make the world a better place for all mankind.

The purpose of the Scripture is not to picture God as a wrathful being just living to pour out suffering upon the world. It rather pictures him as a loving Heavenly Father who sees even when a little sparrow falls to the ground. Jesus explained the purpose of the Law and the Prophets in the sermon on the mount, "Therefore all things that whatsoever ye would that men should do to you, do ye even so to them: for this is the law and the prophets" Matthew 7:12. This is a perspective that we need to regain.

Far from God working to bring judgment upon mankind, the world today is in the grip of a worldwide Satanic conspiracy that is willing to make human life a hell on earth as long as the aims of the conspiracy are advanced. Those suffering are not the perpetrators of evil, but the innocent.

CHAPTER 13

RESTORING THE AMERICAN DREAM

Before we attempt to suggest some answers, it will be helpful first to make a brief assessment of our situation as a nation. First we must realize that, for all practical purposes, the money manipulators and politicians have maneuvered the American people into a position of economic slavery.

In the June 12, 1995 issue of *The New American* Thomas R. Eddlem stated:

> This year's "Tax Freedom Day"—the date on which the average American would finish paying his local, state, and federal taxes if every dollar he earned up to that date went to satisfy his tax obligations—stands at May 6th. But "Cost of Government Day"—which includes the added costs of government borrowing and regulations—will not occur until July 9th.[1]

By 1992 there were more people working for government than working for manufacturing companies in the private sector. There are more farm-bureau workers than farmers, more bank regulators than bankers, more welfare administrators than people on welfare, and more citizens receiving government checks than those paying income taxes.

What people do manage to save is being confiscated by inflation. Remember, inflation is a method of confiscating wealth. Even an inflation rate of only 5% per year will take away the value of everything saved over a 70-year period. This includes the value of insurance and retirement.

The price of a home is tripled because of interest paid on money created out of nothing more than a bookkeeping entry. In rounded numbers, a working couple today buying an average home pays 50% of their income in taxes, 25% for interest, and 5% for inflation, leaving them 20% to live on. At least, it should be just the opposite with 80% to live on and 20% to cover everything else.

All of our money is total fiat, with debt as its only backing. The United States government is now the largest debtor nation in the world with that debt growing about a billion dollars a day. The national debt of about $5 trillion (as of 1996) amounts to over $71,000 for every family of four in the United States.

This growing debt is being used to maneuver the nation under the control of a world bank that will mean world government and the end of our God-given rights protected by the Constitution. It should be obvious to anyone reading these pages that, unless this direction is changed, we face disaster in the not too distant future.

Is there a way out of such a dilemma? There certainly is. However, the answer is not found in government. In his book *Dividing The Wealth: Are You Getting Your Share?* Dr. Howard E. Kershner explained this very well by using postwar West Germany as an example:

> Individuals, not governments, solve problems, overcome difficulties and triumph in the face of disaster. The miracle of German recovery after World War II is a good example of this fact.
>
> After the war the Russian Communists dismantled many industrial plants in Germany and hauled away a great deal of the movable wealth not only from East Germany, but in lesser degree from West Germany as well. This unfortunate country had been more nearly destroyed than any other in Europe. She had suffered the loss of many millions of her strongest young men and had seen a great part of her homes, factories and business buildings destroyed. City after city had been reduced to a mere skeleton and people were living in caves, cellars, quonset huts and three or four families crowded into a dwelling intended for one.
>
> The country was divided into East and West zones and the latter occupied by four hostile powers. In addition, some twelve million refugees from Poland and East Germany were thrust upon West Germany—more than one-quarter of her population.
>
> In spite of all these handicaps, in a few short years Germany became the most prosperous country in Europe, if not in the world. How did this transformation take place? Shortly after the war an official in Bonn gave me the answer, "After the war we had nothing. There was no use to appeal to government for help for we all

knew that the government was penniless. Every German knew that if he wished to survive, he must work. We did. There was no foot dragging. Every man with a job was thankful for it and worked hard to keep it. What you call 'featherbedding' was and is almost unknown in Germany. We were so thankful to have jobs that we did not ask for shorter hours and frequent increases in pay. With farmers and industrial employees working hard, production mounted and employment expanded.

Our government had the good sense to abolish most of the controls and reestablish the free market in which we knew we would be rewarded in proportion to our contribution to the common wealth. In a few short years we were prosperous. As you see, our stores are overflowing with high-quality merchandise, the mark remains stable and among the soundest of the hard currencies. Our gold reserves are more than ample and our domestic and foreign trade are expanding."[2]

Two things that helped make it possible for West Germany to recover were the sale of government-owned industries back to the German people and a return to a sound economic system. Had they listened to American advice, this would not have happened. Dr. Kershner had this to say:

> The United States occupation authorities insisted that the new German government should not balance the budget, but that deficit spending would promote economic recovery and expansion. The man chiefly responsible for the remarkable German recovery was Finance Minister Ludwig Erhard with some coaching from the distinguished economist, Wilhelm Roepke.

> From these men I learned that at one point in the discussion of economic policy, General Lucius Clay, postwar Governor of the U.S. military zone in Germany, remarked to Finance Minister Erhard, "My advisors tell me that you should not try to balance the budget, but should engage in deficit spending." To this Erhard replied, "My advisors tell me the same thing, but we are not going to do it. We intend to balance our budget, not to incur any indebtedness, to avoid inflation and keep the mark stable and sound."[3]

Our own nation was also an example of the results of returning to sound money during the later part of the 19th century until the beginning of the 20th century. In 1875 the Specie Redemption Act was passed requiring that all Greenbacks printed to pay for the Civil War were to be redeemable at face value in gold. As a result, this was one of the greatest periods of growth and prosperity in American history.

The key to a return to sound money is Congress, because Congress makes the laws and Congress can abolish unconstitutional laws. It was Congress that created central banks, and it was Congress that abolished them. It can also abolish the present central bank (the Federal Reserve). Creating the understanding necessary to accomplish this will not be easy, nor will it be accomplished without going through great difficulties. It is too late for an easy way out. The money manipulators have already seen to that. Even if the manipulators don't cause great economic chaos, or a war, as a means of maintaining control over the money system, the unsound system existing today is bound to fail, as have all such systems throughout history.

Our attention must be directed to Congress because Congress has the power to vote the nation into slavery or set it free. Unfortunately, most members of Congress are politicians, whether conservative or liberal, Democrat or Republican, and must be constantly watched, and pressured, to uphold their oath to the Constitution. The measuring stick for their performance is their voting record—their rhetoric means little. The good news is that all members of the House of Representatives serve at the pleasure of their constituents with term limits of 24 months. This means that the American people can change their government any time they choose within 24 months or less.

The nonpartisan educational organization that has been the most successful in publishing and distributing the voting record of House members on key issues is known as Tax Reform Immediately (TRIM). TRIM publishes a report card for every member of Congress several times a year. This is based upon the public record of votes on key spending bills, and is totally unbiased with every legislator being rated on the same bills.

We highly recommend that our readers contact this national organization and find out how you can inform yourself and your neighbors about your representative's record. With this information in hand, the readers can then judge for themselves the performance of their

Congressional representative. The address is TRIM, P.O. Box 8040, Appleton, Wisconsin 54913.

We also recommend that every one interested in more details about banking and the money system order a copy of *The Creature From Jekyll Island: A Second Look at the Federal Reserve* by G. Edward Griffin. This 600-page book is available from American Media, P.O. Box 4646, Westlake Village, CA 91359. Mail order price is $19.50 plus 15% postage and handling. You will find it one of the most thorough works of its kind.

We believe that the American dream will be restored. Depending upon the American people, it could be near total ruin; or it could be rebuilt upon the ashes of our present civilization in the distant future. It may even be rebuilt by another country that profited by our example and became a new hope for the world. Whatever the case, it certainly can be restored.

> In the Carboniferous Epoch we were promised abundance for all,
> By robbing selected Peter to pay for collective Paul;
> But, though we had plenty of money, there was nothing our money could buy,
> And the Gods of the Copybook Headings said: "If you don't work you die." — Kipling.

FOOTNOTES

Chapter 1. Ancient History of Money
1. Hans F. Sennholz, *Age of Inflation* (Appleton WI: Western Islands, 1979), p. 9.
2. G. Edward Griffin, *The Creature From Jekyll Island: A Second Look at the Federal Reserve* (Appleton, WI: American Opinion Publishing, Inc., 1994), p. 146.
3. Sennholz, p. 10.
4. Griffin, p. 150.

Chapter 2. Early History of Banking
1. G. Edward Griffin, *The Creature From Jekyll Island: A Second Look at the Federal Reserve* (Appleton, WI: American Opinion Publishing, Inc., 1994), p. 172

Chapter 3. Rise of a Banking Dynasty
1. Count Egon Caesar Corti, *The Rise Of The House Of Rothschiid* (Belmont, MA: Western Islands, 1972), p. 2
2. Ibid., p. 2-3.
3. Ibid., p. v.
4. Ibid., p. 20.
5. Ibid., p viii-ix
6. Ibid., p. 345.
7. Gary Allen, *None Dare Call It Conispiracy* (Seal Beach, CA: Concord Press, 1971), p.39.
8. Ibid., p. 41.

Chapter 4. The American Colonies and Paper Money
1. G. Edward Griffin, *The Creature From Jekyll Island: A Second Look at the Federal Reserve* (Appleton, WI: American Opinion Publishing, Inc., 1994), p. 310-311.
2. Ibid., p. 314.

Chapter 5. Central Banking in the United States
1. G. Edward Griffin, *The*

Creature From Jekyll Island: A Second Look at the Federal Reserve (Appleton, WI: American Opinion Publishing, Inc., 1994), p. 329.
2. Ibid., p. 329
3. Ibid., p. 331
4. Ibid., p. 348-349.
5. Ibid., p. 354.
6. Ibid., p. 370.
7. Ibid., p. 379.
8. Ibid., p. 374.
9. Ibid., p. 389
10. Ibid., p. 395

Chapter 6. The Federal Reserve System
1. Curtis B. Dall, *FDR.: My Exploited Father-In-Law* (Tulsa, Oklahoma: Christian Crusade Publications, 1968), p. 49.

Chapter 7. Money Buys The Media
1. James Perloff, *The Shadows Of Power: The Council on Foreign Relations And The American Decline* (Appleton, WI: Western Islands 1988), p. 178-179.
2. Ibid., p. 179-180.
3. Ihbd., p. 180-182.
4. Norman Dodd, videotaped interview of, *The Hidden Agenda: Merging America Into World Government*, (Westlake Village, CA: American Media), one hour (VHS)

Chapter 8. The Evils of Unsound Money
1. John F. McManus *Financial Terrorism: Hijacking America Under the Threat of Bankruptcy* (Appleton WI: The John Birch Society, 1993), p. 121.
2. Alan Stang, "Money Talks," *American Opinion*, April, 1975. p. 12.
3. Ibid., p. 11.
4. Hans F. Sennholz, *Age of Inflation* (Appleton, WI: Western Islands, 1979), p. 2.

Chapter 9. The Power of Money to Influence

1. Bryan J. Ellison, *Why We Will Never Win The War On AIDS* (El Cerrito, CA: Inside Story Communications, 1994), P. 232.
2. Peter H. Duesberg "Is AIDS a Hoax?" an address before the United Republicans of California convention, Arcadia, CA April 21, 1990, Hesperia, CA: LTAA Communications
3. Ibid.,
4. Ellison, p. 262
5. Robert W. Lee, "HIV and the AIDS Connection" *The New Ameican*, September 20, 1993. p. 27.
6. Gary Allen, "Common Cause," *American Opinion*, March, 1975. p. 7.
7. Ibid., p. 7.
8. Ibid., p. 8.

Chapter 10. Money Manipulation and Legalized Plunder

1. Mollie Dickenson, "The Real S&L Scandal," *Worth,* September, 1994. p 95
2. Ibid., p. 97.
3. Ibid., p. 97.
4. Ibid., p. 99
5. Daniel Fischel, *Payback: The Conspiracy To Destroy Michael Milken and His Financial Revolution* (New York NY: HarperCollins, 1995), p. 200.
6. Ibid., p. 159.
7. Ibid., p. 59.
8. Ibid., p. 60.
9. Ibid., p. 70.
10. Ibid., p. 158.
11. Ibid., p. 305

Chapter 11. Banking and the New World Order

1. John F. McManus, *Financial Terrorism: Hijacking America Under the Threat of Bankruptcy* (Appleton WI: The John Birch Society, 1993), p. 79.

Footnotes

2. Gary Allen, *Say "No" To the New World Order* (Seal Beach, CA: Concord Press, 1987), p. 241.
3. Jane H. Ingraham, "Worldwide Welfare" *The New American*, September 4, 1995. p. 8
4. Dee Zahner, *The Secret Side of History: Mystery Babylon and the New World Order* (Hesperia, CA: LTAA Communications, 1994), pp. 106-116.
5. Jane H. Ingraham, "Worldwide Welfare" *The New American*, September 4, 1995. p. 6
6. Ibid., p. 8.
7. Carroll Quigley, *Tragedy and Hope* (New York, NY: MacMillan Company, 1966), p. 324.
8. Carroll Quigley, *The Anglo-American Establishment: From Rhodes to Cliveden* (New York: Books in Focus, 1981), pp. ix, 36.
9. Quigley, *Tragedy,* p. 132.

Chapter 12. Regaining a Sound Perspective

1. Joseph M. Canfield, *The Incredible Scofield And His Book* (Vallecito, CA: Ross House Books, 1988), p. 48.
2. Ibid., p. 82-83
3. Ibid., p. 89
4. Ibid., p. 79
5. Charles H. Dyer, *The Rise of Babylon: Sign Of The End Times* (Wheaton, IL: Tyndale House Publishers, Inc. 1991), cover.
6. Ibid., p. i.
7. William F. Jasper, "How to Create an Islamic Enemy" *The New American*, March 21, 1994. p. 15
8. Hal Lindsey, *The Late Great Planet Earth* (New York, NY: Harper Paperbacks, 1992), p. 90.
9. Ibid., p. 91.
10. Ibid., p. 76.

11. Ibid., p. 173.
12. Ibid., p. 173
13. Ibid., p. 134.
14. Hal Lindsey, *Planet Earth—2000 A.D: Will Mankind Survive?* (Palos Verdes, CA: Western Front, Ltd. 1994) p. 91.
15. Ibid., p. 95.
16. Ibid., p. 112.
17. Ibid., p. 171.
18. Ibid., p. 171-172
19. Charles Carlson, "Attacking Islam" *The New American*, March 21, 1994. p. 21
20. Jasper, p. 15
21. Robert L. Pierce, *The Rapture Cult: Religious Zeal and Political Conspiracy* (Signal Mountain, Tenn: 1977), p. 66.

Chapter 13. Restoring the American Dream

1. Thomas R. Eddlem, "A Tax System Overhaul?" *The New American,* June 12, 1995. p. 19
2. Howard E. Kershner, *Dividing The Wealth: Are You Getting Your Share?* (Old Greenwich, CT: Devin-Adair Company, 1971), p. 133-134.
3. Ibid., p. 135.

BIBLIOGRAPHY

Allen, Gary. *Say "No" To the New World Order*. Seal Beach, CA: Concord Press, 1987.

Allen, Gary. "Common Cause," *American Opinion, March 1975*.

Allen, Gary. *None Dare Call It Conspiracy*. Seal Beach, CA: Concord Press, 1971.

Canfield, Joseph M. *The Incredible Scofield and His Book*. Vallecito, CA: Ross House Books, 1988.

Carlson, Charles. "Attacking Islam" *The New American, March 21, 1994*.

Corti, Count Egon Caesar. *The Rise Of The House Of Rothschild*. Belmont, MA: Western Islands, 1972.

Dall, Curtis B. *FDR.: My Exploited Father-In-Law*. Tulsa, Oklahoma: Christian Crusade Publications, 1967.

Dickenson, Mollie. "The Real S&L Scandal" *Worth* September 1994.

Dodd, Norman. (videotaped interview of). *The Hidden Agenda: Merging America Into World Government*. Westlake Village, CA: American Media, (VHS) one hour.

Duesberg, Peter H. "Is AIDS a Hoax?" an address before the United Republicans of California Arcadia, California April 21, 1990. Hesperia, CA: LTAA Communications,

Dyer, Charles H. *The Rise of Babylon: Sign Of The End Time*. Wheaton, IL: Tyndale House Publications. 1991.

Eddlem, Thomas R. "A Tax System Overhaul?" *The New American,* June 12, 1995.

Ellison, Bryan J. *Why We Will Never Win The War On AIDS.* El Cerrito, CA: Inside Story Communications, 1994.

Fischel, Daniel *Payback: The Conspiracy to Destroy Michael Milken and His Financial Revolution* New York, NY: HarperCollins 1995.

Griffin, G. Edward *The Creature From Jekyll Island: A Second Look at the Federal Reserve.* Appleton, WI: American Opinion Publishing, Inc., 1994.

Ingraham, Jane H. "Worldwide Welfare" *The New American,* September 4, 1995.

Jasper, William F. "How to Create an Islamic Enemy" *The New American*, March 21, 1994.

Kershner, Howard E. *Dividing The Wealth: Are You Getting Your Share?* Old Greenwich, CT: Devin-Adair Company, 1971.

Lee, Robert W. "HIV and the AIDS Connection" *The New American,* September 20, 1993.

Lindsey, Hall. *The Late Great Planet Earth.* New York, NY: Harper Paperbacks, 1992.

Lindsey, Hall. *Planet Earth-2000 A.D.: Will Mankind Survive?* Palos Verdes, CA Western Front, Ltd. 1994.

McManus, John F. *Financial Terrorism: Hijacking America Under the Threat of Bankruptcy.* Appleton, WI: The John Birch Society, 1993.

Perloff, James. *The Shadows Of Power: The Council on Foreign Relations And The American Decline.* Appleton, WI: Western Islands 1988.

Pierce, Robert L. *The Rapture Cult: Religious Zeal and Political Conspiracy.* Signal Mountain, Tenn: 1977.

Quigley, Carroll L. *Tragedy and Hope.* New York, NY: MacMillan Company, 1966.

Quigley, Carroll L. *The Anglo-American Establishment: From Rhodes to Cliveden.* New York, NY: Books in Focus, 1981.

Sennholz, Hans F. *Age of Inflation.* Appleton, WI: Western Islands, 1979.

Stang, Alan "Money Talks," *American Opinion,* April, 1975.

INDEX

Abraham: 1,2
Acquired Immune Deficiency Syndrome (AIDS): 72-82,
Age of Inflation: 3, 68
Aldrich Bill: 52
Aldrich, Nelson: 50-51
Allen, Gary: 22, 84, 101
Allied Chemical: 85
American Broadcasting Co.(ABC): 59
American Heritage Dictionary: 2, 69, 86
American Historical Association: 63
American Opinion: 65-66, 84
Ancient Babylon: 118,
Ancient Greece: 7, 8
Ancient Rome: 4
Andrew, Abraham Piatt: 51
Arabs and Islam, The: 123
Articles of Confederation: 27, 29

Azidothymidine (AZT): 76-77, 79, 81
Balfour, Lord Authur: 126
Balfour Declaration: 126,
Bank of Amsterdam: 10
Bank of England: 11-12, 22, 54, 107
Bank of France: 22,
Bank of Germany: 22,
Bank of Hamburg: 11
Bank of North America: 28
Bank of the United States: 34-40
Bankers Trust Company: 51
Barnes, Harry Elmer: 60-61
Beard, Charles: 60-61
Belmont, August: 45, 58
Bennett, John G.: 70
Bickley, George: 45
Biddle, Nicholas: 35, 37-40,

Bismarck, Otto von: 44, 75
Boesky, Ivan: 96
Bolshevik Revolution: 50
Booth, John Wilkes: 45
Bradshaw, Thornton: 59
Bretton Woods: 100
Brinkley, David: 59
British Fabian Society: 101
Brownell, Herbert: 103
Bryan, William Jennings: 53
Bush, George: 119
Byzantine Empire: 7
Cable News Network: 80
Callaway, Oscar: 57
Camdessus, Michel: 103
Canfield, Joseph M.: 112
Carlson, Carole C.: 119
Carlson, Charles: 123
Carnegie Endowment for International Peace: 62
Center for Disease Control (CDC): 73, 74, 122
Cerre, Leontine: 112, 115
Chase Manhattan Bank: 84
China: 24, 66, 120
Civil War: 43-44
Clinton, Bill: 104
Columbia Broadcasting Co.(CBS): 59
Common Cause: 82-85
Communist Manifesto: 56
Cone, Scott: 90
Congressional Record: 57
Constantine: 7
Constitutional Convention: 26, 29
Continental Congress: 28,
Continental, The: 26
Council on Foreign Relations: 53, 58-60, 94, 101-102, 104, 108 119-120, 123-124, 127
Count von Neipperg: 21

Corti, Count Egon Caesar: 13, 17, 21
Creature From Jekyll Island: A Second Look at the Federal Reserve: 4, 25, 31, 135
Daily Capital: 116
Dallas Theological Seminary: 117-119
Dall, Curtis: 55
Darby, John Nelson: 111
Davison, Henry P. 51
Depository Institutions Deregulation and Monetary Control Act: 87
Devin-Adair Company: 61
Dickenson, Mollie: 88
Diocletian: 7
Dispensationalism: 110-111, 117
Dividing The Wealth: Are You Getting Your Share?: 131
Dixon, Donald: 91
Dodd, Norman: 62
Dole, Bob: 104
Dow Jones Industrial Average: 94
Drexel Burnham Lambert: 92-94, 97-98
Duane, William: 38
Duesberg, Peter: H. 78-80, 82
Dyer, Charles H.: 118
Eddlem, Thomas: 129
Ehrlich, Paul: 120
Electoral College: 37-38
Ellison, Bryan: 74, 80
Emancipation Proclamation: 43
England: 20, 25
England's Midland Bank: 107
Erhard, Ludwig: 132
Ex Post Facto Law: 95-96
Federal Home Loan Bank Board: 86
Federal Home Loan Banks: 86
Federal Reserve Act: 49, 52, 53

Index

Federal Reserve, The: 49, 50, 52-56, 66, 87, 133
Federal Saving and Loan Insurance Corporation: 86
Fiat money: 24-26, 70-71
Financial Institutions Reform, Recovery and Enforcement Act (FIRREA): 88-*89*
Financial Terrorism: Hijacking America Under the Threat of Bankruptcy: 64, 100
First Bank of the United States: 29-33
First National Bank of New York: *51*
Fischel, Daniel: 91, 95-98
Ford, Gerald: 67
Ford Motor Company: 85
Foreign Affairs: 123
Forrester, Izola: 45
Fortune: 59
Foundation for New Era Philanthropy: 70
Founding Fathers: 27, 38
Fractional-Reserve Banking: 8-9, 11, 41
Francis, Donald: 74
Francis of Austria: 17,
Frankfurt, Germany: 13, 20
French Revolution: 17-18, 66
Friedman, Alan: 119
Gaebelein, Arno C.: 111
Gallo, Robert: 72-73
Gardner, John: 83-84
Garn-St. Germain Depository Institutions Act of 1982: 87
General von Estorff: 15
Germania Saving and Loan: 90
Germany: 13, 131-132
Gingrich, Newt: 104
Glass-Owen Bill: 49
Goldman Sachs: 103
Good Morning America: 80

Graham, Katharine: 58
Greenbacks: 46, 133
Griffin, G. Edward: 4, 6, 10, 25-26, 31, 36, 44, 47-48, 135
Group for the Scientific Reappraisal of the HIV/AIDS Hypothesis: 81
Guggenheim Foundation: 63
Hamilton, Alexander: 29, 30
Hammurabi's Code: 2
Health and Human Services: 72
Heckler, Mararet: 72
Henry Regnery Company: 61
High-Yield Bonds: 88, 93-92, 94, 98
Hitler, Adolf: 50, 67, 127
Hoppe, Donald: 65
House Banking Committee: 119
House, Edward Mandel: 53, 102, 125, 127
House of Rothschild: 13, 16,
Human Immunodeficiency Virus (HIV): 72-75, 77-81,
Hussein, Saddam: 118-119
Illuminati: 45
In common Cause: 83
Incredible Scofield and His Book, The: 112
Inflation: 25, 68, 130
Ingraham, Jane: 104
Ingalls, John: 112, 114
Insider Trading: 95
Insider Trading Sanctions Act of 1984 (ITSA): 95
Insider Trading and Securities Fraud Enforcement Act of 1988: (ITSFEA) 95
International Labor Organization: 76
International Monetary Fund (IMF): 100-102 105
Iraq: 118-119
Islam: 122-124

Index

Israel: 11, 120, 125-127
Jackson, Andrew: 35, 37-38, 40,
James, Jesse: 45
Jasper, William: 119, 123
Jefferson, Thomas: 30,
Jekyll Island: 50, 52
J.P. Morgan Company: 51
Kalischer, Zvi Hirsch: 125
Kansas City Journal: 113
Kershner, Howard: 131-132
Keynes, John Maynard: 64-65, 67, 101, 127
Kipling: 135
Knights of the Golden Circle: 45-46
Koch's Postulates: 77
Koop, C. Everett: 74
Koppel, Ted: 59
Kuhn, Loeb & Company: 50-51, 58, 85
Landmark Land Company: 90

Larry King Live: 80
Late Great Planet Earth, The: 119
Laurence, Richard: 40
Lee, Robert W.: 82
Legal-tender laws: 24, 26
Lenin: 64-65, 67, 76
Life: 59
Life of C. I. Scofield, The: 112
Lincoln, Abraham: 43-45
Lincoln Saving and Loan: 91
Lindsey, Hal: 119-122
London: 20
Look: 119
Lord Alfred Milner: 127
Lotus Club: 115
Louise, Marie: 21
Luce, Henry: 58
Macdonald, Margaret: 111
Manchester Guardian: 125
Mao Tse-tung: 120
Marco Polo: 24
Mark of the Beast: 99

Marx, Karl: 56, 66, 102, 125
Massachusetts: 25
Matthews, Herbert: 58
McManus, John: 64, 100
Menger: Carl, 3
Metternich: 21
Mexico: 103-104
Meyer, Eugene: 58
Miller, Judith: 123
Milner, Lord Alfred: *107-108,*
Milken, Michael: *91-92, 94, 97-98*
Money: 59
Montagnier, Luc: 73
Morgan, Jack: 52
Morgan, J.P.: 50-53, 57-58
Morris, Edward: 90
Morris, Robert: 28, 31
NAFTA: 104
Naples: 20
Napoleon: 11, 18-21
National Banking Act: 46
National Broadcasting Co.(NBC): 59

National City Bank of New York: 51
National Debt: 130
New American, The: 82, 104, 119, 122-123, 129
Newsweek: 77
New York Times: 58, 118
New World Order: 124
Niagara Bible Conferences: 111
None Dare Call it Conspiracy: 21
Norman, Montagu: 54
Norton, Charles: 51
O'Brien, Robert: 89
Ochs, Alfred: 58
Office of Research Integrity: 73
Office of Thrift Supervison: 88, 90
Old Testament: 1
Oxford University: 107-108, 111-112, 117
Oxford University Press: 112
Ozone: 122
Palestine: 125-127

Index

Paley, William: 59
Payback: The Conspiracy to Destroy Michael Milken and His Financial Revolution: 91
Peabody, George: 51
People: 59
Percy, Major Henry: 20
Persian Gulf War: 119
Peso, the: 103
Philadelphia: 26
Polo, Marco: 24
Post: 58
Planet Earth- 2000 A.D.: Will Mankind Survive?: 121-122
Plymouth Brethern: 111
Princeton/Newport: 97
Quigley, Carroll: 22, 106-108
Racketeer Influenced and Corrupt Organizations Act (RICO): 97
Radio Corporation of America (RCA): 59
Rather, Dan: 59

Reece, Carrol: 62
Reece Committee: 62, 63
Reichsbank: 50
Regan, Jay: 97
Resolution Trust Corp. (RTC): 88, 90
Rhodes, Cecil: 106, 108
Rhodes Scholarships: 107-108
Rhodes Secret Society 126-127:
Rise of Babylon: Sign of the End Time: *118*
Rise of the House of Rothschild, The: 13, 17
Rockefeller Brother's Fund: 84
Rockefeller Foundation: 60, 62
Rockefeller, David: 84, 93, 102
Rockefeller, John D. III: 84
Rockefeller, John D. Jr.: 51
Rockfeller, Nelson: 84
Roepke, Wilhelm: 132.

Roman Empire: 6-7 65-66
Rome and Jerusalem: 125
Roosevelt, Franklin D.: 60, 76, 100
Roosevelt, Teddy: 52
Rothschild, Alphonse: 51
Rothschild, Baron Edmond de: 125
Rothschild, James: 15,
Rothschild, Lord Nathaniel: 126
Rothschild, Meyer Amschel: 14-16, 21,
Rothschild, Nathan: 15, 19. 20
Rothschild, Solomom: 15
Rothschilds: 13-23, 25, 31, 44-45, 51-52, 48-49, 84, .107
Round Table Groups: 108
Rubin, Robert: 104
Ruskin, John: 108
Russell, Bertrand: 120
Russia: 66

Sanders, George: 45
Sarnoff, David: 59
Saturday Evening Post: 59
Savings and Loan Crisis (S&L): 86-88, 90-93
Say "No" To The New World Order: 101
Schiff, Jacob: 50, 58
Scofield, Cyrus I.: 111-112, 115-117,
Scofield Reference Bible: 111-112
Scott, C.P.: 125
Seasons, The: 45
Securities and Exchange Commission (SEC): 95
Second Bank of the United States: 34-35, 38-39,
Secret Side of History: Mystery Babylon and the New World Order: 110
Sennholz, Hans: 3-4, 68
Socialized Medicine: 75

Index

Social Security Department: 76
Specie Redemption Act: 133
Spider's Web: The Secret of How the White House Illegally Armed Iraq: 119
Sports Illustrated: 59
Stock Parking: 96
Strong, Benjamin: 51
Taft, William Howard: 52
Tax Freedom Day: 129
Tax Reform Immediately (TRIM): 134
Thomas, Charles: *81*
This One Mad Act: 45
Time: 58, 119
Toynbee Hall: *107*
Tragedy and Hope: 106
Trilateral Commission: 94, 102
Truman, Harry: 102
Trumbull, Charles: 112, 115,
United Nations, The: 105-106, 120, 122, 124, 126

United States Bank Notes: 46, 47
United States Constitution: 27, 95
United States General Accounting Office: 92
Vandelip, Frank: 50, 51
Venice: 9-10
Venna: 20
Vernon Saving and Loan: 91
Wall Street: 54-55, 103
Wall Street Journal: 93
War of 1812: 33
Warburg, Felix: 49
Warburg, Max: 50
Warburg, Paul: 49-51
Washington, George: 26,
Washington Post: 58
Waterloo: 19
Webster, Daniel: 37
Weizmann, Chaim: 125
Wellington: 19, 20,
Whip Inflation Now (WIN): 67
White, Harry Dexter: 101-102

153

Why We Will Never Win The War On AIDS: 74
Wildcat Banks: 33
William of Hesse: 20-21
William, Prince of Hanau: 15
Willing, Thomas: 31
Wilson, Woodrow: 52-53, 60, 125
Wolf, George: 39
World Bank: 102, 105, 127
World Health Organization: 74, 122
Worth: 89
Wyman, Thomas H.: 59
Young America: 45
Zedillo, Ernesto: 103
Zionists Movement: 125-126

ABOUT THE AUTHOR

Dee Zahner is a graduate of what is now Bartlesville Wesleyan College where he majored in theology. He is also a graduate of the Los Angeles County Sheriff's Academy for Reserve Officers and served as a reserve deputy sheriff for ten years. For several years he served as a lay minister at the Little Chapel of the Canyon in the San Gabriel Mountains in Southern California.

In 1982 he became the producer and host of "Let's Talk About America" a weekly series of radio interviews that were eventually heard in 37 states on radio or cassette tapes. "Let's Talk About America" has been aired on seven radio stations in California.

In addition to *The Secret Side of Money: A History of Manipulation,* he is also the author of *The Secret Side of History: Mystery Babylon and the New World Order* and *Gringo and the Coconut* a true human interest story in English and Spanish with a screenplay included.

A small businessman for the past 27 years, he is the owner of LTAA Communications a book publishing and audio production company in Southern California.

ADDITIONAL COPIES OF THIS BOOK

Single copies $10.00 plus $2.00 postage & handling

40% discount on quantity purchase
Five or more copies $6.00 each postpaid

California residents add 7.75% sales tax

order from

LTAA Communications
P.O. Box 403092
Hesperia, CA 92345

or

call toll-free
(800) 962-2084

ANOTHER BOOK YOU WON'T WANT TO MISS

THE SECRET SIDE OF HISTORY
MYSTERY BABYLON AND THE NEW WORLD ORDER
by Dee Zahner

"A number of books have been written in past decades that demonstrate parallels between events in recent history and certain passages in Scripture. *The Secret Side of History* belongs among the best of such works since author Dee Zahner possesses an excellent command of the scriptural and historical material with which he deals. Moreover, he builds his story — which is really the story of the eternal battle between good and evil — on the foundation of the research of a number of outstanding writers, historians, and researchers of the past, to which he adds significant augmentations from the present, combining all into a thoroughly readable book."

— THE NEW AMERICAN
DECEMBER 12, 1994

216 PAGE PAPERBACK BOOK
$10.00 plus $2.00 shipping & handling
money back guarantee of satisfaction

ORDER FROM
LTAA COMMUNICATIONS
P.O. BOX 403092
HESPERIA, CA 92345
FOR FREE INFORMATION CALL
(800) 962-2084

AUDIO BOOKS

on

THE SECRET SIDE OF HISTORY

and

THE SECRET SIDE OF MONEY

- Three C90 cassettes in attractive album
- Quality cassettes with unlimited warranty
- Chapter index included
- Money back guarantee of satisfaction

$15.00 each postpaid

ORDER FROM
LTAA COMMUNICATIONS
P. O. BOX 403092
HESPERIA, CA 92345

FOR FREE INFORMATION CALL
(800) 962-2084

AN IDEAL GIFT FOR ANY OCCASION

GRINGO AND THE COCONUT

A TRUE STORY IN ENGLISH AND SPANISH WITH SCREENPLAY by Dee Zahner

Gringo and the Coconut is the kind of delightful true story that you will want to share with all of your family. Seldom does a story appeal to readers of every background from eight to eighty, but *Gringo and the Coconut* is a rare exception. Written in English and Spanish, it makes an ideal gift for any occasion.

The story begins when the author, a Caucasian businessman in his middle fifties, finds a teenaged Mexican girl on a city street carrying much of her earthly possessions in a knapsack and in need of most of the things in life that we take for granted. Little did either party dream that sharing a warm meal in a nearby restaurant would be the beginning of a life long father daughter relationship that would conquer a mountain of trials and build a love and trust strong enough to overcome the boundaries of race, culture, age, and everything else that hinders mutual friendship and understanding.

The good times, the sad times, the tragedies, and triumphs will make you want to laugh and cry as you travel through this unusual real life adventure.

To add to your reading pleasure, a screenplay (in English) based on the story is included in the book. The screenplay, like the book, contains all the comedy, tragedy, and suspense needed to make you want to keep turning the pages. There is never a dull moment with *Gringo and the Coconut.* One Hollywood agency labeled it, "A terrific story."

The Spanish version of the story is beautifully written and enjoyed by all ages among those who read Spanish. Their comments have been most gratifying.

271 PAGE PAPERBACK IN ENGLISH AND
SPANISH WITH SCREENPLAY
$10.00 plus $2.00 postage & handling
money back guarantee

ORDER FROM
LTAA COMMUNICATIONS
P.O. BOX 403092
HESPERIA, CA 92345

FOR FREE INFORMATION CALL
(800) 962-2084

ORDER FORM

ITEM	Qnty	Amount

Sub Total _____
CA tax _____
Shipping _____
TOTAL _____

TO ORDER BY PHONE CALL (800) 962-2084
SEND TO
ADDRESS
CITY   STATE   ZIP
Make checks payable to LTAA Communications P.O. Box 403092, Hesperia, CA 92345